Past & Present

Monika Mann

Past & Present

TRANSLATED FROM THE GERMAN
BY FRANCES F. REID AND RUTH HEIN

St Martin's Press

NEW YORK

First published in Germany by Kindler Verlag
under the title *Vergangenes und Gegenwärtiges*

FOR TONI

My father died on August twelfth, nineteen hundred and fifty-five. I have put a cross at the point I had reached in my writing when the mournful news was brought to me.

M. M.

Book One

[I]

I live on an island. Here it is quiet, and the people are thoughtful. City dwellers don't do much thinking because noise kills thought and because they are preoccupied with dodging cars and escaping the hands of thieves. But on my island, as I said, the people think.

The other day an old, taciturn fisherman asked me, "What is life?" At first his question struck me as a little silly and useless, and in answer I stared at him blankly. But his question seemed to echo in the silence. What is life? He must have been trying to trap me: he knew more about it than I. Living on this quiet island, he had given it much thought. I felt cornered and beset and said, just to regain my freedom, "A gift." The fisherman must have expected anything but this—he looked angry. I apologized, and added in a rush, "A battle, an expression of will, a test——" shook my head and admitted that none of this was to the point, that I didn't know, and I begged him to tell me. Now he seemed truly angry and his clenched fist thrust at the air as though seeking some kind of release, or break-through. Then his hand relaxed and he pointed into the distance. He knew better than I: he pointed across the bright, wide sea, as though the answer lay there. His look cleared and softened, and I understood. He meant that life is the liberation of the self.

Visionaries and poets are given to doubt and to precipitous action because of an inner urgency that works upon them; but the prosaic, cool, practical man is more successful in life than the artist, for in the artist exists something that I call "un-life." Alice in Wonderland wanted a year of 366 days, so that she could also have an "un-birthday." This irrational, or super-rational, element is also part of the poet's being. I belong to a family that, as far back as I can remember, has been driven by this un-life. A strong, self-conscious spirit, urgently striving for release, pervaded our warm, middle-class home like a specter. Long before I had the slightest understanding of what the soul of an artist might be, I experienced its secret turmoil like that of a natural force. And long before I had read a book or knew what art is, I sensed that this organic power reached far into the world.

I may have noticed, too, that our house, wreathed in wild vines and climbing roses, for all its rural seclusion mirrored the complex great world; and not only because letters and visitors poured in from everywhere, but because of my father's character. In spite of his living withdrawn, concentrated on himself, his mind remained open to the world, united with it. Nothing in our calm, plain existence of that time pointed to the wandering life in store for me, for I grew up in the half-light of worldly solitude. Although we were intellectually receptive to the outer world, there was in our home a deep self-sufficiency.

The strong, controlled personality of my father and my mother's dynamic temperament joined to create an atmosphere against which all outside life grew pale. The household's whole troop of brothers, sisters, friends, servants, and animals did its part in extending and securing this peculiar solidarity. Yes,

❀❀❀

I grew up in a very dynamic home, and its sound and ring is loud in my memory.

The twenty years I spent in my parents' house might as well have been two millennia, for there is something basic to childhood and youth that extends the phenomenon of time to infinity. We are wrapped and muffled in time, which only later becomes transparent. The child, at heart, does not believe in recurrence; or, in his blind faith in the present, experiences an eternity between one event and the next. When Mother said, "Stop playing now and go to bed, tomorrow is another day," the truth of her statement was by no means guaranteed. First of all there was the night, an unpredictable, unforeseeable span, to which we were totally surrendered. It was easy for Mother to talk; far better to be thorough, to finish today's game today. For the same reason, a good-night kiss was to us a serious and momentous parting.

So I sat as long as possible on Mama's lap every evening, to experience fully the sweetness of the moment. I even think I may have intimidated her with teasing tenderness and sometimes overstepped the "as-long-as-possible," so that Papa—who at that time wore a fat mustache—was compelled to bring about our separation by a forceful word.

I mustn't forget to mention that Papa's mustache was usually trimmed quite short, and that every change—for a few days he was clean-shaven—signified betrayal, as a near-fanatic liking for uniformity and continuity always characterized his being. So it may have been, too, that my childish or elfin excesses rather irritated him.

On Sunday morning, Mama held "open house"— that is, my sister and I were allowed to slip into her bed. It was wide, and made of ivory-colored wood decorated with carving. Mama wore a very long nightgown, with flounces at the neck and wrists and, although made of the finest linen, it was reminiscent of the gown worn by the grandmother in Little Red Riding Hood. Two braids of dark hair— which she wore coiled around her head during the day—spread over the large pillows; these, too, were made of linen, with open-work embroidery.

She wished us a good morning in a deep, husky, caressing voice. It was very pleasant first to stand barefoot on the thick bearskin rug, or sometimes to kneel, before creeping in under the cornflower-blue

❀❀❀

comforter and to breathe in the peculiarly astringent fragrance of the bedclothes—smelling, as it seemed, of the very scent of security.

A few shafts of morning light came into the room through the two windows and the door which opened onto a verandah where, every afternoon, Mama would rest (in winter wrapped in a large fur rug). The sound of church bells now and then was wafted to us from the town. A peaceful half-light filled my mother's room, which for me was always associated with attractively chaotic plenty and seemed the center of life itself. On the dressing table with the three-faced mirror there lay, between the cut-glass bottles and crystal and silver boxes, the bills—perhaps already paid—for coal and milk. On the velvet chaise longue, striped in green and blue, lay a heap of red crochet wool, volumes of Maupassant, Zola, and Josef Ponten. The dresser was heaped with a colorful load of letters and manuscripts, a huge sewing bag of lilac-colored leather, innumerable family photographs, keys, a large satin pincushion covered with pretty old brooches, a vase of roses and a confusion of telephone lists, menu cards, and Christmas presents made by childish hands. The elegant writing-table was weighed down by two typewriters, my brothers' Latin books, Russian dictionaries, and boxes of bitter, cat's tongue chocolates.

Am I exaggerating when I add that, from morning till night, my mother's bedroom was the scene of both chaos and our life's center? A magnetic attraction seemed to turn it into the heart of the house. If a red-faced governess didn't have some complaint to make, a workman would want his instructions, or a maid would come in for some money; if Papa wasn't calling us to go with him for a walk, then Mother's tailor would arrive, his face pale and a little mad, to fit a new robe, or a child would interrupt in need of comforting.

We took our friends into my mother's bedroom; even the dogs found their way there. All telephoning was done from there, whether it was an order for twenty-eight Wiener Schnitzel or a gay long-distance conversation with Gerhart Hauptmann. True, he insisted on exchanging a few words with Papa personally, so that my mother—quite contrary to the general rule—would have the telephone call switched over to the study. There Papa could send forth his "Grüss Gott" and "Hello" and his mild laugh, while it was never clear to us whether the

❀❀❀

embarrassed politeness in his voice was caused by the instrument, or the rarity of telephoning at all, or whether it was a tribute to his venerable friend and colleague.

And now the telephone was silent, and, giggling and whispering, we told each other our dreams, and the tumult of Mother's daily round was buried in the greenish light of Sunday morning.

❀❀❀

Each weekday morning at seven, my brothers and
sisters and I met in the bathroom for a "cat wash."
After a breakfast of bran bread and synthetic honey
we said good-by to Mama and set off for school.
The others took the trolley halfway across town,
but I had only to climb over a fence to reach my
"little school." My father—who was usually just
throwing open his bedroom shutters as we left the
house and would smile down at us—often asked me
how things were going at the little school. And
though—or because—the phrase was apt, my feelings were deeply hurt. After all, didn't the small
private school in the next garden have proper
benches, and a desk for the teacher? And wasn't
it true that the teacher, though her voice was fluting

and sweet, was not averse to using a delicate Spanish cane on any of her six young pupils—though she
turned chalk white? I can't remember who it was,
my father or my brothers and sisters, who declared
that she often kissed the top of my head, thus making it impossible to take seriously its claim to be a
proper school. I was very glad indeed when I was
old enough to go to public school and become part
of the "great world."

The public school was attended by perhaps a
thousand children, who filled the gray building
with their clamor. I was passionately fond of this
school, I was in love with it—possibly because it represented a new and wonderful contrast to the atmosphere of home, where separate personalities
were so strongly preserved. Whenever I started out
for school—on a November morning, a cold drizzle
shrouding the streets—our home seemed to dissolve
into nothing. The school satchel sat on my back like
a hump under my green cape which fluttered in the
wet wind, and as I stuck my nose heavenward from
under my hood and frowning slightly, with impertinent earnestness, lost myself in the observation of
the common herd. Workers making their way toward factories, sullen or whistling; a girl in black,

❀❀❀

tripping with sour coquetry toward her office; men who even at that early hour were shoveling coal into a cellar; the greengrocer, using a long hook to open the metal shutter of his shop; a high-spirited undergraduate taking a taxi to the university; the street cleaner, lethargically sweeping up the rotting leaves; many boys and girls on bicycles, clutching briefcases; and I—we all formed a mysterious unity in the damp and chilly morning light.

And having passed through the park and its hillock of leafless, sodden shrubs, I crossed the big open square and darted through the school portal like a brownie; I was wholly absorbed in its prosy magic. My swarming fellow students in the halls and on the stairs, in the lecture rooms and playgrounds, seemed to be controlled and governed by the spirit of the herd, which we all served. Although I really knew that it was the school porter who rang the bell, it seemed to me to be the summons of that same herd spirit, and so its notes sounded each day anew with universal force—compelling, releasing—penetrating me to the marrow.

If I may boast of having been in this public school, a brilliant pupil—indeed, by far the best in my class, quite contrary to all my other school years—it was

❀❀❀

probably because this new experience of being a part of the herd quite simply inspired me.

At that time my friend was a girl named Sturm, Babette. She wore a shirtlike dress of hessian cloth and great wooden clogs, a long braid hung down her narrow back, and she talked the argot of the cabdrivers. Although I was simultaneously attracted to a princely boy with white socks and doelike eyes, whose speech was like the twittering of birds (especially in his use of sibilants, in such words as "sun" and "sweet" and "shorn"), it was the language of the cabbies—quite in keeping with the revolutionary post-war times—that took possession of me and exposed me to mockery at home.

Not only the Sturmbabettes, but we girls at home also wore hessian dresses and wooden clogs, and at meals we quarrelled like seagulls over an extra piece of bread. Had Mama not put her entire energy into the acquisition of a few extra eggs or a little additional milk (she was not above cultivating friendly relations with arrogant black marketeers or from making long cross-country bicycle trips in all sorts of weather) we children would have suffered from malnutrition, and simply would not have grown up. At the family dinner table, presided over by Papa, our

❀❀❀

14

gull-like cries had to be muffled to a greedy hissing,
which was not easy for us when we sighted a delicious, pink, frothy dessert. Papa was not a bit re-
luctant to eat these unnourishing concoctions, his
face dignified, his silver spoon moving majestically.

We were helped somewhat through these dark,
lean times by the maintenance of order and good
manners. Even our coarse dresses had a certain chic,
and we learned how to step softly in our clogs. Our
short haircuts, washed with synthetic soap, were
never allowed to go uncombed; even genuine want
would have been graciously hidden or surmounted
in a family committed to good manners and a respect
for human dignity. Thus I grew up amid a sort of
fictitious order and well-being which, although it
was good for me, made me in the face of occasional
obstacles, all the more sensitive.

The poor who often were hungry and cold, and
those who had suffered from the war, were driven
to crime and despair, and our "mansion" was frequently an object of envy and dislike. It was dreadful when the housemaid was finally unmasked as
a thief and taken away by the police (she had
previously entertained dubious fiancés below-stairs,
who complained that the dog had torn their trousers

❀❀❀

and with dire threats demanded new suits from my mother). But this was nothing compared with the night when a man shot himself outside our garden door. Our feeling of terror and incomprehension was hardly tempered by the fact that the suicide had missed his aim, and was soon after his deed entertained by Papa with brandy. It was a winter night and as we were having late tea, we heard a shot close to us in the darkness. Papa went out immediately, expecting to find a man dying. In the dim light of the gas street lamp a man—his eyes turned up, muttering a woman's name—leaned against our bloodstained fence. The excitable young stranger's arm wound had no serious consequences, and he might even have found his way back to life without Papa's brandy. But it was a chilling incident and my gentle, withdrawn father was there to help, not as an effusive Good Samaritan, but with a calm, determined readiness born of understanding and necessity. He, the distant one—whom the English might characterize as "aloof"—could always be counted on when there was a basic human need.

❀❀❀

were done. He intimated further that we should courageously attract that which was possibly impossible, to welcome it. The world consisted of the accessible, real, factual, of all that was limited; but also of all that was created by faith, all that was true and boundless. Only the "dry-as-dust" rationalist lived and was governed by the first; the romantic and enthusiast, by the second. But to combine the two ways, to weave them together with simple decency, that was the aim of the whole man. What made him whole was that he loosely controlled both the possible and the impossible, reality and fantasy, the factual and the true, the restricted and the unrestrained, the bounded and the free—offsetting this duality by devoting all his will toward giving them equal play. The fact, for example, that at one time my father attended séances and regarded with fascinated interest the tricks of spiritualists (subsequently unmasked) indicated the catholicity of his nature and was rather a sign of tolerance than of a dark poetic soul. Yes, at that time Papa was in a very spiritualistic mood, and twice a week he and a neighboring professor—who was the person who had "seduced" Papa—took the trolley to the meetings. My mother, a "mathematical mind," could not accept such doctrines, but she accepted his belief, just as she never failed him in any matter requiring adaptability and deep tactfulness.

For us children black-magic games were at this period the only ones—if "games" they could be called. I was convinced that a spirit "spoke" from the table around which we sat holding hands in the dark room. The gentle raising of the table leg would cause the spirit to tap out its ghostly prophesies, interrupted now and again by stubborn silence, in spite of our concentrated entreaties; and it was only this intense concentration that kept my teeth from chattering. After all, we were in direct touch with the "other world"—the awe of it held me transfixed.

Besides this "table-turning" among friends, my brother—a year older than I—joined me in a midnight rendezvous in the attic. At five minutes to twelve, stifling the ringing of the alarm clock under the feather bed, we stole with fluttering hearts up into the attic under the rafters. My brother, barefoot, dressed like me in a short flannel shirt, held a lighted candle to show me the way. I followed. The attic was, even in the daytime, far from cozy; it was the site of so much discarded living. Mice scrambled among the relics of bygone times, portraits of an-

cestors smiled mildly through the cobwebby dim-
ness, and there was either a humid heat in summer
or as now, a penetrating cold. This night white sheets
hung from lines and swayed gently in the light of
the candle. My brother disappeared behind a sheet,
and finding myself alone, I gave a small cry. Frightened, my brother let the candle go out; total fear
filled me, against which I armed myself with heroic
strength. In fact, terror so stiffened me that I felt
scorn when I heard a soft moaning in a corner. It
wasn't frightening enough: now I thirsted for real
ghost orgies of which, thanks to my feverish heroism,
I felt I ought not to be deprived.

In this state the fear of a child is so powerful that
his imagination reaches the limit of creativity. I can
still recall happily our "spirit creation" of that night.
Between the moonlit sheets there first appeared to
our spellbound eyes the foaming head of a horse,
then a riding boot in a stirrup, a swaying white tunic
and, finally, the large, pale face of Napoleon, the
world-tyrant. His coat collar was turned up, his hair
clung to his white forehead and, right hand on his
heart, he gazed into the distance with black, mocking
eyes over which a deep wrinkle was sculptured. My
brother asked him, stuttering and lisping in broken

❀❀❀

French, whether the time might be near when he (my brother) would be ruler of the world. At this the splendidly curved lips of the magnificent one trembled and cast forth a hollow-sounding "oui." Then the picture dissolved. We returned to our beds, but it was a long time before our senses relaxed and we were again received into the deep sleep of childhood. The following morning we did not know whether we had dreamed all this or had experienced it, but the open attic door and a sheet lying on the ground assured us that Napoleon had truly appeared to us.

The opaqueness of time that the child—the believer in the present—experiences makes the changing of seasons appear to him as something sharply defined, as a series of deep incisions into life. When the last flowers had faded, the last leaves fallen, when the fire was lit in the hall, then it meant farewell, farewell to the autumn days—so often warm and glowing—on which we bicycled along the river or strolled through our English garden. Autumn was particularly beautiful in our city and full of an almost deceptive splendor. What dark, unreal weeks were to follow? When would it return?

When the first snowflakes fell, that was called winter, winter for an immeasurable time. Our garden looked dreary until slowly its melancholy aspect cleared—even took on a look of peacefulness—when at last it was covered with snow and lay open to the winter sunshine. On the bare, icy branches of beeches symmetrically grouped around the square of lawn the sparrows hopped about, and sometimes we saw a squirrel with a beautiful bushy, red-brown tail. The small clipped hedges beside the rose beds, the young fir trees close to the edge, the lilac, the chestnut, and the pergola—all were so white; and though our garden was rather small, and its pattern a little too symmetrical, in its dreamy whiteness it now took on a certain scenic grandeur framed by the park silently surrounding it.

There my father could be seen sauntering with his dog around noon, when other families were already having dinner—we ourselves ate later. Dressed in hat, fur coat, and warm overshoes, and carrying a cane, he moved with visible enjoyment, through the neat outdoor scene. He would walk alone on the snow-covered river bank, sometimes calling the dog away from his gull-chasing with a high, clear whistle.

On Sundays we played on the nearby slopes and

hillsides with hundreds of sledding children, each trying to excel the others in daring. Often we did not return until evening, and often we were bruised. We left our boots in the cellar, and, although this was forbidden, sat in our stocking feet at the family tea table which stood in a snug corner of the dining room. Behind the closed folding doors, through which the odor of cigar smoke penetrated, we could hear the sound of Papa clearing his throat. My brother and I started wrestling noisily, the teacups rattled—and Papa, who had issued from his study more in consternation than in anger, had to use thundering words and physical force to separate us as we rolled on the floor like a pack of fighting dogs. Soon afterward we were playing with puppets or gluing and pasting away at Christmas presents.

❀❀❀

[IV]

Christmas: that meant a universe where time passed in magical suspense and activity, but with slow steps. Would everything be ready in time, and would we be sufficient unto the high festival? Anticipation and apprehension were in balance.

Between the bouts of pasting and pinning and painting, embroidering and knitting, writing music and poetry, there were the excursions into town, where the brightly decorated shops, full of sporting goods, toys, and books, shone in the snowy dusk.

Then came the feast of St. Nicholas, the baking of gingerbread, the fairy-tale play in the little Opera House, the school parties, the Christmas Oratorio; and all that culminated in—but did not end with—Christmas Eve. Parties at the houses of our grand-

parents and uncles and friends followed on New
Year's Eve and New Year's Day and the feast of the
Three Kings. Only then was it time to "retrench"
and to turn from an intoxication of happiness to
ordinary life.

And that, too, was good—as good as a piece of
plain bread after an orgy of candy. All in all, at
bottom everything was good. For the child, cling as
he may to "now" and "today," nevertheless finally
buries them deep in "yesterday," so that he rises un-
trammelled on the morrow, full of new energy. Com-
pensation is his strong suit, and with marvelous clev-
erness he takes new heart from the flow of life to arm
himself against whatever has gone amiss. So we also
buried that time of joy and gladly exchanged it for
the daily round. And yet, in our heart of hearts, we
lived all year for the Christmas celebration: all
yearning, all deliverance lay in this glowing goal.
What could be greater than to share the divine—
made manifest to us by the scent of pines and glitter
—yes, truly to be included in the divine?

Once, in a school Christmas play, I was assigned
the part of an angel. And, wearing a white robe
which reached to my toes, two large golden wings,
a golden crown of stars on my head, and singing

❀❀❀

with outstretched arms, I was not acting—I *was* an angel! I can testify to this still, for I jumped off a very high table (disguised as a cloud) without hurting myself in the slightest—a feat I could not have accomplished in my mortal state.

In our family the Christmas traditions were carefully kept and honored. A large part of the credit for this must go to my mother who with the solicitude of a mother-bird brought so many magnificent things into the nest; yet the most powerful influence was my father's reverence for festival. There was nothing of religious orthodoxy in this feeling; it was an indefinable emotional response and a devotion in the face of the feast as such, in its original form the celebration of Christ's birth. It was a deep hesitation, in which the Highest—everything—and the self found confirmation. The recurrent feast was a glowing focus of love and creation, and its ceremony was essential to them. Small wonder if in our home the feast was exceptionally festive.

And so the winter passed, and spring broke upon us in its circling return. Sunny breezes came from the south, and the river, swollen and gay with melted snow from the mountains, ran between banks covered with primroses and violets. The branches

❀❀❀

brought forth pussy willows, and yellow buds appeared on many tender, light-green twigs, opening
up with almost shameless rapidity after a warm
shower of rain. Then came a storm of wind and hail.
It poured, it blew, it snowed, and the yellow buds
lay limp on the ground. It was sad, certainly, but in
the midst of life's colorful chaos we did not question
it. Soon pink and white flowers would appear, almond and cherry blossoms, the splendid candles of
the chestnuts, and later on lilacs, roses, and flowering
limes. Those first yellow flowers were but a tiny pre-
view of the great blossoming to come.

In the spring nothing seemed serious to us. We ran
about with wet feet until we were too hot, and then
we sat down on a stone and let the wind blow
through us. The next day we were feverish. But even
that wasn't very serious. It was a swift, spring fever,
between intoxication and pain. The scent of jasmine
drifted in through the open windows of the sick
room, and in the universal impatience recovery came
quickly.

Then—I don't know now whether it was in that
time of urging and thrusting and sprouting, or if it
fell simply in the midst of our young existence—our

aunt died. She was my father's sister and my god-mother. And it was the first time that we children had been asked to attend the funeral of a relative. It seems strange that death touches the child in the same way that it moves me today. The irrevocable, incomprehensible aspect of mortality seized me then as it does now.

I cannot recall the details, but I still see the rela-tives and friends, dressed in black, forming an empty semicircle. It was a vaulted, empty hall filled with chalky light in which the black figures stood in their semicircle, their faces pale and stricken. While the final rites of death were being performed—symbol-ically, mechanically, not touching the reality of the thing—the image of the departed impressed itself upon our minds. The large picture hat on the ash-blond upswept hair; the translucent, drawn face with the blue, veiled eyes, the high, soft forehead, the nose slightly too large and a little curved, the small mouth from which would spring a sudden, gentle laugh while a rosy blush spread over the alabaster face; the helpless hands . . . this person, spinsterish and yet fairylike, vain and distracted, but most of all familiar—where was she? How many times I had sat on her lap while she had asked me,

❀❀❀

looking at me with her veiled blue eyes, "Are you my little angel?" to which I had assented, shyly roguish. To this day I have the silver fork and spoon she gave me as a baptismal present, and her memory; but from that day on I have not had my beloved godmother—and that is not right. It wasn't right, or it couldn't be true, and it numbed me. And now, suddenly, in the semicircle of mourners I caught sight of her picture hat, and the tears streamed down my face.

As always the family met at the lunch table. The conversation was general. My father was pale. He acted as "ordinary" as possible; for he wished to spare us. And he seemed to seek protection with us. He was upset, he suffered. Suffered all the more because the pastor's speech had lasted long past its apportiond time and prevented him from delivering his planned address. Now he carried these words of farewell around with him still, a dull load. But perhaps this was good. Perhaps it was good to endure and to be silent, to leave everything unspoken in the face of the unspeakable.

❀❀❀

[V]

Next to Christmas we lived for the long summer vacation. Even though school provided us with a certain moral stability, and though we recognized the absolute necessity for this formative social and ethical foundation—on which we even leaned with considerable pride and a touch of affection—nevertheless our real life took place in the summer holidays. From secrecy to openness, from compulsion to individual ambition, from the law to liberty—these were the transitions we had to make in the changeover from school to vacation.

I used to have one teacher who, at the beginning of the autumn term, would abandon the usual grammar lesson to ask each pupil about his experiences during the holidays. And it was a joy to hear this room of severity and duty echo with happy tales of youthful adventures in forests and mountains.

Summer: there was something almost festive about the heat. Our clothes were light and thin, and our motions were measured. In the afternoons Papa, with a handkerchief over his face, used to lie in a deck chair in the shade of the birches. The air was still and full. I would gather the rose petals that lay in colorful carpets on the sunken lawn, and sit under the chestnut tree, where it was beautifully dark and cool. Humming very softly, I made patterns of the petals on the table.

After tea we would run about on the grass in our blue-and-white-striped bathing suits, and our parents, to our great delight, would take turns spraying us with a large garden hose.

After sundown we could see Papa, in his white linen suit, sitting at his desk. We saw him through the folding doors of his study, which opened out onto the terrace where the wild roses grew, and which were kept shut against the heat during the day. Before going to bed we rummaged through our toys and books, discussing what to take along on our vacation trip. There was a lot to be arranged, considered, provided for, in the few days before we were to leave.

Then there we were—seven of us in a third-class compartment, with a great deal of luggage and a large collie dog, rolling toward the mountains. During the three-hour journey in the slow local train we sucked almost continuously on the fruit drops which would otherwise melt in our pockets, counted the telegraph poles, and looked at the familiar places —woods, meadows, and farms—which we had passed last year and all the previous years.

That was the beginning of a long holiday from school. And as this freedom belonged to us, we gave ourselves up to it. The child's behavior is naturally attuned to freedom's beautiful, dangerous realm; he knows how to deal with liberty. He is helped by instinct, as well as by a love of order and a deep realism. Indeed, the astonishing aspect of children's experiences and pastimes is their profound factuality. And the more imaginative the child, the stronger and purer is this tendency to concreteness. How cold and methodical is the child's absorption in his games of make-believe. That was no dog, but an enchanted prince; this, no garden but a kingdom, and there stood not my brother but the chieftain of

❀❀❀

a robber band. The game was a success when we believed in it, and in order to believe we had to maintain a calculated reserve. Overexcitement or an intoxicated involvement in our fantasy would quickly cast us back upon reality, and boredom would be the victor. I was not I, I was a witch: and to raise myself from the status of myself to the status of the witch, I must, with cool resolution, sacrifice myself. In general, the child's interest in objects was predominantly factual, serious, unself-conscious.

As a result, time was never wasted; we were constantly educating ourselves. I could sit for hours under a tree watching the ants, and at the same time I would be unconsciously examining my own life. Without being aware of it, I compared their puny activities with much larger ones. I was fascinated by their movements. First I watched the moving mass, then I would try to follow a single ant. This was not easy, for an individual disappeared again so quickly in the crowd. I looked for some sort of identifying marks, but the ants were all the same. What were they doing? They hurried back and forth over the small patch of friable earth, impelled by the rhythm of existence, and sometimes a few of them would disappear entirely into cracks and crevices. Their

❀❀❀

articulated, almost muscular, tiny bodies seemed tireless, their busy being divinely in tune with life itself.

We helped the farmer with his haying, picked raspberries, swam in the swampy forest pool, played in our garden, and strolled on the roughly cobbled street of the village with its old, brightly painted houses, its wells and wayside shrines. Yet at the heart of our carefree existence we were surely sensible of that rhythm that allows for no halting and drives every human being into a well-defined path. And our pretty country house in its large garden, between fields and woods, surrounded by old trees and beds of fine dahlias and with a view of the small, dark, and distantly blue mountains, was dominated by the rhythmic force of my father's personality.

Here, as at home, Papa had a study with his books and "memorabilia" and regular hours of work. But whether he played tennis with Mama in the garden, climbed hills with us, or read aloud to us—sometimes a reading in his comfortable study would be interrupted by great cracks of thunder—or whether he took the highly temperamental collie for a walk in the woods (when the dog would turn around seven times in a frenzy of delight): all his actions were

❀❀❀

strictly planned. "Papa is playing tennis," meant that
nothing short of a violent storm could deter him,
and that we had to respect this fact. There was
nothing tyrannical or cantankerous about this; it
simply meant that his decisions and actions were
governed by the twin star of desire and duty. The
following incident became a standing joke between
us: We always took our midday meal at half past
one. Copper finger bowls and silver knife-rests lent
an air of special distinction to the simple country
meal which was served by our cheerful, buxom
maid. I, by far the youngest of the family, sat beside Papa, raised in my chair by cushions. After the
customary soup (to this day Papa's favorite food),
fish soufflé, a light dessert, and a glass of beer, my
father lit a cigarette. I could feel him looking at
me through the haze of blue smoke. More exactly—
he was looking at my hair, which was long, silky,
golden brown, and curly. Attractive hair. Provoca-
tive hair. I pretended not to notice his glance and
the slight twitching of his hand, and turned my eyes
to the flowers in the middle of the table. Then I felt
an imperceptible movement in my hair and, before
I knew what was happening, the knife-rest had become hopelessly entangled in my curls. I didn't know

[VI]

The dark-green pine wood with its scents and se-
crets; the wide meadows filled with lush clover, but-
tercups, bluebells, and the humming of bees; the
mountains veiled in dramatic thunderclouds or glowing at sunset; the long, steady, life-giving country
rain, after which frogs croaked in the marshy grass
and we ran barefoot on the flooded paths looking for
snails to roast; the friendly country children; the
colorful market street lined with cozy, familiar
shops, where on Sundays bearded men in lederhosen
danced clog dances on a platform garlanded with
flowers—without these it would be impossible to
imagine our childhood, our summer happiness.

Down at the bottom of time there still exist, unchanged, the graceful, rustic house with its paneled

walls and carpeted floors, the golden-brown water of the forest pool, the wild raspberry bushes at the edge of the wood where every day, accompanied by Mama and wearing light blue peasant dresses, we vied with each other to see who could gather the most berries. With her dark braids around her head in a "Gretchen" hairdo and wearing a long white linen dress with Bulgarian hand-embroidery, my mother resembled a refined, exotic peasant woman. The endless games with our collie, Motz, in the large garden. . . .

His must be the place of honor in time's court. He had assumed the role of our trusted friend and guardian, an impressive figure with thick coat and faithful look. A hut in the garden where tools, deck chairs, and tennis rackets were kept was the palace of the great and powerful Sultan Motz who, dressed up in a ragged yellow bathrobe and crowned with ivy, could punish his subjects by invoking thunderstorms, but also knew how to preserve them from all the world's ills. But when Motz's gait became too unsteady, his eyes too wild, and his mouth began to foam, he had to be shot. One noon we heard three quick reports. And we knew: now he is dead.

❀❀❀

We mourned, and the following summer we would sit around his grave, which we had decorated with ivy and dahlias and a handsome stone.

Inherent in my father's life force—that splendid yet merciless force which bore us all along—was music. Music always played a major part in our lives, though in an undefinable, unique way. We never, for example, played chamber music, as did many "educated" families; our father would sometimes improvise on our Blüthner grand piano before dinner, that was all. His commitment to music was at once submissive and striving, suffering and combatant—it was embodied in his art and his life.

There have been many music-loving poets (Hermann Hesse, Franz Werfel, Romain Rolland, etc.), but there may never have been another artist who utilized his layman's knowledge (for Papa is still a layman in music) of a second, essentially foreign and never practiced art form in such a deep and total manner as Papa. For that reason he not only entered into the musical world but attracted it to him. Conductors, composers, musicologists always had a special affection for him and elected him, as it were,

❀❀❀

to honorary membership in their domain. But had Papa been a "musician manqué" instead of a writer whose very roots were tied to music, real musicians would not have had this admiration for him. I consider this a remarkable, unique phenomenon, and would not wish it to be interpreted simply as a filial paean.

My grandfather on my mother's side, a great Wagner admirer who had had—no matter how legendary it may sound—personal contact at Bayreuth with the operatic giant, enriched our childhood and adolescence by performing for us every Sunday. The elegant, slightly baroque, highly gifted old man sat on the dais in his noble music room and, together with a friend, played two-piano arrangements of extracts from the *Ring, Tristan, Parsifal, The Flying Dutchman, Lohengrin, Meistersinger,* and *Die Feen,* while we, seated on gold-bordered velvet wall-benches, listened, benumbed and entranced.

Our grandmother, who was totally unmusical but had a grand gift instead for reading aloud from Dickens, performed a purely decorative function at these musicales. A very dignified ornament she was, though, as she sat very erect, wearing lace, her beautiful face white with powder, her curls silvery, her

❀❀❀

ringed hand holding a lorgnette with which she rapped our fingers whenever these, in our ecstasy, happened to touch the velvet pillows.

Because Wagner's music first impressed itself upon me in the stately confines of my grandparents' home, by which we were much awed, but where we also received many reproofs and slapped hands, I still associate its essence with both glory and terror. The high, cathedral-like ceilings decorated with frescoes, the walls hung with tapestries, the damask armchairs: the ghostly splendor of the ancestral house re-echoed with the sweet yet virile, hypnotic power of the Ride of Valkyries, the Good Friday Spell, the Liebestod, the Geistersturm, magnificent and extraordinary. I was about to say that Wagner, with his mighty, theatrical spirit, is terribly suitable for children—but he is just too mighty for a child. That Papa's asceticism is coupled with Wagnerian pomp must be explained by the proverb, "opposites attract." His deep, loving connoisseurship of Wagner probably stems not least from the child in Papa, his love of theater, and here especially for the powerful musical theater. That one day Papa referred to Wagner with a smile as "that old rogue" is significant, for it testifies to his somewhat guilty love for the com-

poser, a love which Papa has no intention of banish-
ing from his life.

Besides going to concerts and operas, we had
record-playing evenings at home. Papa operated the
hand-wound phonograph with great patience and
care; the traditional repertoire—consisting, for example, of songs by Schubert, Strauss, and Wolf, a
Tschaikovsky piano concerto, arias from Verdi,
Weber overtures, Beethoven's *Fifth*, Mozart's *Eine
Kleine Nachtmusik*, Brahms' *First*, Donizetti's *Don
Pasquale*, the final chorus from the *St. Matthew
Passion*—echoed through the paneled hall with its
three windows draped in dark-red silk. We listened
sitting by the hearth in the firelight, some of us in
armchairs, some on the red staircase. We considered
Papa an expert at cranking the victrola and felt that,
with natural authority, he created calm and unity.
His way of listening was infectious—a special way:
he listened with his whole being, and his receptivity
was in itself a creative act.

It was with the births of the "little ones"—though
I was still little myself—that my childhood came to
an end. The nestling of the family until then, I be-

gan to experience maternal feelings for the two children born after me. Whenever I could I would go into the nursery, where I watched all the baby-care procedures with the utmost interest until I learned to do them myself. It became my passion to feed the babies, change them, cuddle them, lull them to sleep, and entertain them. I was sympathetic toward their teething and learning to walk, and directed all my efforts to teaching them to talk. I had the romantic idea of training them to pronounce the letter "r" far forward on their tongues, and it was a real triumph when after cunning, patient exercising they brought forth a flawless pronunciation of my own coinage, "Tshintadigore." Since they managed to throw out the word with lazy elegance and exotic swing, I made up my mind to try further, still more daring experiments.

Our previous appearance, always somewhat fanciful, with artist's garb and pageboy haircuts, which had netted us in the streets a frequent, "But who are you?", was altered by the babies' coming to something more adult and serious. Now my brothers had short haircuts, we girls wore braids, and all in all it was a more ordinary, more anonymous exist-

Book Two

[I]

I did not do well at the "School for Young Ladies"
(what an undemocratic name!). I was refractory and
lazy, traits which, in the school's undisciplined and
unencouraging atmosphere, led to disaster. Except
for French, German, physical education, and singing, none of my courses interested me in the least;
I tried to play hooky from them, and to escape them
by tomboyish pranks. Let me be frank: the hour
for Bible lessons I usually passed in the large clothes
closet, where my girl friend and I gossiped and ate
chocolate bars while the pastor's long, black-clad
legs darkened the wardrobe door like a thunder-
cloud. Our favorite retreat from the natural-history
classroom was the bicycle cellar, where we performed
a tinkling bell concert and, at the approach of any

footsteps, slipped into a kind of cavern where coals and bits of broken furniture were stored.

I was in love with my physics professor, a sentiment he repaid with sadism. Whenever I could not answer one of his questions he left me standing—instead of sending me back to my seat with a reprimand and a failing grade—until I cried. All this time he would stand quite close to me and, with his hands folded behind his back and his face nearly touching mine, look at me searchingly and steadily. No one in the classroom laughed; the other girls rather held their breath during this cruel game—until one or another tried, by raising her hand urgently, to release me from his spell. That was the physics professor, he of the English suits, the blue eyes, and the blond Vandyke beard—whom I continued, nevertheless, steadfastly to adore.

But the man responsible for the dramatic dénouement—for my dismissal—was the history professor. Thinking back on it now, I see him as a spider enticing a fly into his web. He was far too familiar with us. He would overstep the bounds of dignity and, when he had lured us far enough into impropriety, would suddenly close his net with the accusation that our behavior was most unbecoming. Then he would shake his obscenely fat head so that he flushed a dark red, and roll his eyes, and I thought I could hear a dreadful muttering in his thick black beard. This sort of thing reached such dangerous extremes that one fine day I made a hurried exit from a school I detested in any case.

At this point things took a turn for the better: I was sent to a so-called country school, where school and life were blended into a harmonious whole. The teacher was both friend and mentor, and, as a result of the day-long discipline, we became self-reliant and developed a sense of responsibility we had not known before.

Home had been like a nest, where the protection and authority of our parents fundamentally controlled our actions. But this school was like a state, a nation with rules, conditions, and laws, with comprehensive opportunities for distinguishing oneself, for making oneself ridiculous, for progress and success. Here we were not "children," or "pupils"; but "persons." And just this was new and wholesome.

It was especially good for those of us who, as girls, ran the danger of being too dependent. Now everything was treated as a whole: the pupils were friends, fellow beings, whose approval was as necessary as

❀❀❀

that of those in authority. Though in a very simple way, duty and happiness and kindness went hand in hand. Honor and friendship were better not trifled with; loyalty and deep devotion to the community were insisted upon, and softness was scorned. Anyone who told a lie was shunned for weeks, and no one was allowed to speak to him. Since the community was all, he became a leper.

The former convent—converted into a boarding-school by one of the south German princes—was situated in an attractive, fertile district. Surrounded by orchards, meadows, woods, and vineyards, the school buildings adjoined the royal residence, which in turn abutted on the village and the church buildings. Behind the school was the large playing field where the traditional hockey matches and Olympic games took place; these, following the Greek and English patterns, were an important aspect of our life.

The girls lived in the south wing, in Spartan rooms for four, each furnished with folding beds, an iron stove, and a table for study. The boys led a communal existence in the north wing. The cell-like rooms, some of them overlooking the Prince's garden and others the countryside, had a peculiar charm, particularly when it was white and frosty outside, the stove was glowing, and the girls—ranging from twelve to seventeen in age, with one of them as "room leader"—sat together within.

Lights were put out at nine o'clock, and at half past six in the morning the oddly hoarse voice of the house porter woke us in time for running exercises. Naturally we didn't go to sleep at nine o'clock, but entertained ourselves with all kinds of pranks and make-believe, at which I often managed to provoke laughter. The devoted principal of the school had the loving respect of all the children, no matter what their antecedents. The school brought together in a single community aristocrats, commoners, Jews, and possibly even illegitimate children, and together they formed a free, cosmopolitan little world.

Guiding this world of sports, music, nature study, crafts, and play were the slogans "camaraderie" and "human dignity." The strong and penetrating spirit of the school did not lose its hold on its one-time pupils even over the decades: just recently I encountered one of the school's "boys," and we found our way back into that world quite effortlessly. The horrifying piece of world history that had intervened did not prevent me from recognizing in this man the

❀❀❀

handsome fourteen-year-old of Spanish ancestry with whom at one time I had played music and dug potatoes (and whose exotic good looks, by the way, served as my father's model for the "young Joseph"). And as we addressed each other naturally with the familiar "du," we suddenly were reabsorbed into that world.

While the German state schools of that time smelled of sadism, anti-semitism, and Nazism, the spirit of the country schools was a humane one, and I can only be grateful to that bearded monster for having exiled me from the lyceum for "Young Ladies."

I made two friendships there that I think of today. One was a haggard and bespectacled girl who seemed somehow unable to manage her long-limbed body. She was thoroughly intelligent and deeply kind, and—I don't know why—she was drawn to me; was, as we used to say, foolish about me. Although her appearance was far from classical, she was a great student of Latin and Greek, read a great deal and—in spite of her too serious, forlorn, and almost tragic manner—she had a great sense of humor. When you got to know her she turned out to be very amusing. And she could be overcome with laughter

—I can still see and hear her chortling and gasping with mirth, the tears running down her cheeks under her glasses so that she had to take them off; and, strangely, when she removed her glasses I always felt very sorry for her: there was something so naked, so wounded about her. The boys teased her, but they liked her. It was recognized that she was fair and if need be would always help anyone out of a sticky spot.

We not only sat next to each other in classes and at meals, but shared the same room, sang together in the choir, and were together during the afternoons set aside for nature lessons and bookbinding. We both elected to be backs on the hockey team, we ran races together (she could always beat me, for she ran astonishingly fast), and we kept together during paper chases in the deep woods.

[II]

That was one of my friendships. The other was with a Jewish orphan from Berlin whom God had blessed with great musical talent. This eleven-year-old boy —very Jewish, almost Arabian in appearance—looked like a graceful street urchin. His intelligent, delicate face, framed by thick black curls, bore a slightly ironic smile, a smile already full of knowledge and yet retaining an entrancing innocence.

Since he had a tendency to chilly hands, he nearly always wore woolen gloves knitted for him by his grandmother in Berlin. This grandmother seemed to be his best and only attachment in this world, and he mentioned her with secretive but slightly mocking tenderness—just as the boy himself emanated a strange aura of mystery and loving scorn.

Because of his delicacy and "pianist's hands" he was excused from a number of duties, and while the others were at games he could often be seen wandering about alone in a shabby woolen cape. But most of the time he sat at the piano, and we often crowded around and admired him. Talent in action; skill always testifies to maturity, yet how could this be reconciled with this exotic, undersized "beggar" with the blue-veined hands? When he played these hands seemed to undergo a transformation—to become spiritualized, ennobled, to infuse the keys themselves with life. And his street Arab's face was suddenly illuminated with vivid expression somewhere between impertinent gaiety and melancholy delight. He improvised operatic potpourris, flawless in dynamic and harmonic composition; supplemented his piano performance with vocal imitations of woodwinds and brasses, and bass and coloratura singing; galloped across the keyboard like a runaway horse; lost himself in lyrical passages, his head laid back, his face dreamy, his arms and fingers long and caressing. What a devil he was! And he was not a child prodigy who appeared on a platform dressed in velvet, and to whom the audience threw kisses and flowers—he was our fellow-student, our friend.

The music teacher treated him like his own son. We used to see them walking up and down the cloistered halls or in the park, the "father's" hand on the boy's shoulder. The older man was a type out of E. T. A. Hoffmann. With his mane of hair flying around his head, his sensitive hands played "Kreisleriana" with more of the Schumann spirit than I have heard since. Although his romantic appearance seemed at variance with the school's outdoor spirit, he was very popular. I experienced a surge of happiness whenever I ran into this eccentric, touching couple, and by and by I succeeded in attaching myself to them. Often I listened to them talk about Schumann, Chopin and Brahms, Mozart and Beethoven; but sometimes both were silent. I was allowed to share their instruction and accompany them into the realm of music. The handsome young Spaniard and another boy joined us, and we formed a small group. Often when the day's schedule was read off we were called out for a "musical afternoon." In the "grand-pianoed" salon, with tea and cake, we were instructed by "Bandmaster Kreisler" in the history of music, style exercises, improvisation, and sight-reading, and it was absolutely wonderful. My thorough success with Schumann's "Kinderszenen" at the school concert persuaded me to undertake serious study, which years later I abandoned. Today, on my island, I play only the phonograph. "Only"?

I can't avoid a digression in praise of long-playing records. There is hardly a greater pleasure than to listen to them at home. To sit in an armchair, looking out at flowering gardens, sky, rocks, and sea; listening, say, to the Budapest playing a Mozart quartet—how's that? The rendition is so marvelously close to the live performance—three dimensional, without interruption or extraneous noise. The act of listening in these familiar surroundings is pure and blessed. The listener's part in bringing about the performance—no matter how petty and mechanical—together with the selection of the record give rise to a feeling of "doing." In a way there is participation, one is responsible for the concert. And by the way: that taciturn old fisherman did not believe in music. He opposed it, denied it, even passionately. It made me think of atheists who negate a Nothing and build their creed upon this paradox—not knowing that with the double negative they create an affirmative. He listens to a Mozart quartet. Suddenly he exclaims,

❀❀❀

"What does it mean?" Despairingly, he asks, "What is it, what does it represent?" He demands content and meaning, he wants the notes to tell him of their origin and aim through some recognizable pattern. He listens. "What does it mean?" he cries. "What is it telling me?" he wants to know, and he makes it sound like a challenge. How am I to fight it out with him? "Well, a song with words is probably more in your line," I say. Program music, background music (as in the movies), dance music, all of these create an atmosphere, a feeling, stimulate motion. But this quartet, what does it mean? I stumble over my words: "Abstract speech—the fusion of the individual heart with the heart of the universe; from the universal heart springs rhythm—rhythm already contains sound, in which other sounds are mingled— harmony and melody join in—the air is full of music, all you have to do is wake it from its silence—human genius needs only to reach into the air and wake the sounds, invent them, discover them, join them in a mosaic of sound that will ring on . . ." He laughs derisively: "It doesn't make sense. I don't understand."

"The ear carries the vibrations in the air to the

brain," I stumble on, "and because of this the brain begins to soar, animated as with vintage wine, and it transfers this effect to the other organs and the senses; and soon the whole being soars in its turn, and is dissolved in the spheres of music. Music has a different meaning for each of us, just as champagne or opium affects us differently. Some people become melancholy, solemn, and sentimental, while others grow careless and aggressive, and still others generous, compassionate, and tender." But in everyone capable of hearing music, it awakens to some degree an awareness of the self's participation in the universe. There has been much discussion of the moral power of music, but who can say whether its influence is good or evil? I dare say that its power transcends such concepts and values, and stems rather from the human longing for eternity, of which it seems an echo. But man's creative power, man's genius, forever takes its impetus from all areas, high and low, divine and daemonic. I'm trying to get at the roots of this fisherman's anger. Evidently he suspects the existence of something overwhelming; one doesn't revolt against trivialities.

Northern music is foreign to the sensitive Italian,

he suspects depths in it that he cannot reach, loses contact half way, protests, condemns. I add, "You mustn't look for images in music. Even if it is the transfigured voice of nature—wind, thunder, bird song—it is nevertheless transformed a hundred times. It is unrecognizable. Rather, imagine that you find music in the air, much as fishermen find pearls in the sea or miners gold in the earth."

He snorts mockingly, and the sound becomes a whistling noise, a snatch of song without words. "Well, what meaning has that?" I ask him lightly, "your whistling?" "None," he answers, "it's the answer to all our chatter." "All right," I say. "And by the way," I add, "our music is a very young art, it flowered quickly and didn't develop further; perhaps it has even degenerated. So there is a possibility that this art will end, that there won't be any more music one of these fine days."

"Pity," he mumbles, and goes on whistling. . . .

One of the most delightful events while I was at the school was our (fragmentary) performance of *The Marriage of Figaro,* in which the voice teacher took the part of the Countess, the musical boy was the Count, the prodigy played the page Cherubino, and I was Susanna. Our genuine enthusiasm was probably the best thing about it. Young and ignorant though I then was, this performance of Mozart made a lasting impression on me. Quite simply, the public singing and acting of this music was an elevating experience for a child. We rehearsed with industry and pleasure—I sang the letter scene in my dreams—and finally we were ready for the great night.

Invitations had been sent to the villagers, the mayor, the pastor, the doctor, and neighboring farmers and gentry. The sitting room contained innumerable chairs and a curtained platform. The make-up man from the theater in a small town nearby had come to do our hair and faces. I felt the full responsibility and enchantment of a miniature diva. I was got up in a crinoline with three underskirts, a laced waist, a wig, and layers of pink and white face paint.

Just before the performance I was rather bewildered by a remark of my brother's (he was also a boarder at the school). He declared I looked like "Aunt Mimmi." Aunt Mimmi—God bless her—was our stately, even too stately, aunt—but I was Susanna, Susanna! I threw him a "You're crazy" and asked him to cross his fingers for me. He did, and everything went off splendidly. I can truly say that it was one of the high points of my youth. "Press and public" agreed in prophesying a dazzling operatic career for me—but the prophecy was never fulfilled.

❀❀❀

to cry—we saw it, saw it ever more clearly, until finally we reached the place where a fine straight fir tree stood in a blaze of brightness, covered with hundreds of lights, ornaments and presents; and how then, when all were there, we had sung Christmas carols, and how the cold, stiff forest had been warmed. . . .

And how the following morning we had all departed in different directions, and how we had had such a long wait at the junction for our connection, which had been late because of the snow; how we had sat for a long time on hard benches, with our suitcases between our knees and our caps drawn down over our ears, looking out through the dimmed windowpanes and shivering with cold; and how finally a low rumble under our feet had heralded the approach of the train, and how the train had suddenly roared into the station, filling the snowy air with black smoke and noise; and how we had had to stand up the whole way in the crowded, freezing corridor—and how good it was to be home now.

Had we remained at home we would not have noticed the changes in ourselves, but now, after an absence of months, our matured senses experienced everything in a new way. Nothing was

❁ ❁ ❁

changed, yet everything was altered. Our own inner transformation was transferred to objects, so differently did we perceive them. Our consciousness of familiar objects had been intensified and changed as a result of our separation from them; and to recover these things unchanged but not the same, produced in us at once a feeling of gratitude and of curious examination.

This consciousness of the familiar marked the beginning of our maturity. Here began the difficulties and the glories, here began real life—a life so much under our father's influence that we did not know whether to think it a curse or a blessing.

That period of my life was probably the most difficult, since on the one hand I was strongly dependent on external influences, and on the other I was subject to strong individualistic impulses. Hence I lived in a constantly fluctuating balance between these outer and inner forces.

We all know how at that age there is a tendency to imitate, how the young person raves and mimics, confronts values and people moodily and capriciously, and juggles with ideals; yet how at the same time the genuine self emerges—how what is individual and real seeks anchor in a sea of curiosity,

❀❀❀

passion, and unrest. For this reason it is difficult, looking back, to recapture that chaotic and meaningful time. Too much and too little can be said about it; its conflicts, conspiracies, and complexes, its undefined drives and lack of form, glide through one's hands, escape one's memory. We feel something like shame about it, and at the same time are too proud to abandon it.

Besides, it is hard to say when that period of life begins and ends, since we are not divided into compartments, and the drama of life is not broken into acts but is a constant outspinning of the web of self. But there are strands in this web which stand out and glow; the great song contains notes which resolve themselves into one dominant chord which has never been sounded before, but which now will ring out in ever new modulations, and upon which all the future will depend.

Love is one such dominant chord. And though it created once more a complete disorder in my life, it marked the beginning too of a new order and confidence. It brought to an end, as it were, the great inhaling and began the exhaling, externalization and self-dispersion, the will to expression and form. Everything became more definite, clearer, more ar-

❀❀❀

ticulate; and as our bonds with home were loosened and we turned outward, the world became smaller and more comprehensible.

It would hardly fit the tenor of these pages for me to discuss my first love. And anyway I'm sure it was just like yours, and yours. . . . Just this: we saw each other daily, and, after parting, each of us would write a letter to reach the other on the day of our next meeting. This overlapping of real and epistolary emotion was strange. The documentary evidence of yesterday heightened the experience of today; the letters were like tangible pearls on the invisible strand which joined us. And because it was so very long ago, I suppose I may say that he was the son of an Allgäu farmer and was named Charly.

Incidentally I believe that love, no matter how personal and terrifying it may seem, is a purely ancillary phenomenon, since it is the carrier of life. And because I believe this, I call after my first love (Who knows whether he can hear me?): "I salute you."

❀❀❀

[IV]

Our town derived much of its charm and gaiety from its closeness to the country—it was a sort of rural metropolis. In it strangers and natives, sportsmen and artists, townsfolk and bohemians, peasants and aristocrats rubbed shoulders; it was a town that managed, by its cosmopolitan geniality, to blend a diversity of groups. The trolley conductor joked with the long-haired poet; Baron So-and-So of Castle So-and-So spoke the local dialect, and had the cheery, slightly bearish manner of the countryside. The patrician debutante married the daredevil ski champion; the Catholic peasant lad who carved crucifixes went about with the exotic prince of Bohemia, and the innkeeper's daughter laughed herself into the good graces of the young philosopher.

Past & Present

It was an easy-going, generous town where everyone understood everyone else and everyone felt at home. This sincerity—the candid criticism and naive solidarity—had an Italianate touch, which was echoed by certain Florentine-type buildings. And the presence of these southern elements in our rugged mountain town created a charming juxtaposition.

In our home the babies had already grown up: the older children were students or were engaged to be married, and the oldest were traveling about the world. What with the constant turnover of house guests and the turmoil attending every sort of social function, our house might well have been taken for a hotel. But, in the last analysis, it preserved its private, basically serene, aspect. This agitation was only on the surface; under it, with well-meaning irony, ruled the spirit of the house—a spirit at once adaptable and domineering, which no commotion could affect.

My father dominated in a passive way—it was less his actions than his being that determined us. He was a conductor who had no need of waving his baton but ruled the orchestra by the sheer fact of his presence. A twitch of the shoulder or eyelid, a

slight tapping of one foot, and the mildly errant
oboist was immediately sent back to his measure.
Further, the improvisation was a very modern one,
in which everyone could play what he liked as long
as certain ground rules were observed. The performance had to be very bad before. . . . For example, Papa sent money to Tokyo or Honolulu,
which had in no way been postulated, when improvised cries for help in cable form had arrived from
the "big children."

He took part in our wild and eccentric merry-
making in his own way. It would not have carried
much weight if he had joined in the emasculated
Negro dances which we enjoyed. But he did stand
in the doorway between his work room and the hall,
his arms crossed, a smile on his lips, and his patent-
leather slipper tapping rhythmically. As he nodded
to a good-looking boy or girl who danced past, the
eyes behind his thin gold-rimmed glasses would
deepen for a moment. When the perilous Charleston
was over, Papa would personally put on a record of
a Strauss waltz, which Mother would dance to with
the handsomest young man of the evening—the same
young man who, in "Disorder and Early Sorrow,"
causes Ellie so much heartache. I wore my straw-

berry-pink "art nouveau" dress, and Papa said, "If Charly could see this!"

In "Pücki," a small green, gilt-edged, limp-leather notebook which Mama filled with stories about me, it is recorded that Papa remarked, "Moni is roguish, nothing more." This "nothing more" indicates that, though Papa had pronounced against my being anything "more," he had considered the possibility. The question remains, what is this heightened roguishness? A great rogue in my eyes is for example Puck, the spirit of the forests. His kingdom is the whispering glades, where the enchanting imp, nature's sprite, passes his days, divinely undiscovered. . . . Papa considered this possibility and rejected it. But I must confess that I've great sympathy with woodland spirits, and a love for divinely undiscovered nature.

Out in our countryside: no village in sight, only a single farm, a field, a trackless forest, and an indistinct little path embarked on quite unawares. . . . There, when the sun cast its evening light and sank, blood red, into a furrow; when dusk followed and the silence shrilled with uneasiness, and when under the naked foot the earth was black and ardent as a young widow, when a thousand steeds galloped through the air, foaming at the mouth. . . . Final silvery sheen of daylight, fading at last, when night embraced the wood, the field, the farm, and there was rest—relief from light, so that the whole world was a free shadow, through which one moved like a dancer, an elf, who weds all space to all time. . . . And then, if you laid your cheek against rough bark and could not go on, could not—if one could only be a sleeping elf in the resinous aroma of forgetfulness!

In my fiery-red little sports car, the "Opel baby," it didn't take me long to get out into the country. On a fine evening it might occur to me to drive to one of the enchanting mountain lakes nearby. Beauty, especially the beauty of nature, fills me at first with a kind of defenselessness—I feel assaulted by it. Even while struggling against its power I try to find in it that "something more" I seek. I try to imbue it with meaning; there must be a meaning in beauty, for only then can I hold my own against it. And as I absorbed them into myself, shape and color, wind and cloud became a wordless poem, a wordless prayer, a living poesy in which I swam and climbed and picked flowers, and walked on my hands, and grew brown as a berry.

But one of the very best things was gliding on skis through the snowscape. It was the joy of this sport, combined with the clean magic of the snowy fir woods, the white mountain silhouettes, the orderly turmoil of a snowstorm and the bell-like blue of a sunny winter sky that gladdened me. The deep, victorious downward rush, the easy, feathery plunge through the glittering elements, gliding along in the bluish twilight, the fantastic purity of winter: these were to me the epitome of youth and beauty.

❀❀❀

[V]

I can imagine that even the heart of a doddering old
man might swell, awakening to this whiteness, and
that under the ringing sky his limbs might stretch,
and his blinking eyes grow light and gay. Yes, he
might even grow a little carefree, the old fellow,
put a red stocking cap on his silver hair, and very
softly hop from one foot to the other. And a group
of children—though their noses run from cold they
are laughing lightly—might crowd around him and,
singing and whistling, tie a mask over his face so
that now he looks like a crocodile. The children
might be wearing colorful paper hats and masks that
disguise them as cats and clowns and pixies, and
someone might be playing a barrel organ, and another ringing a cowbell, and a baby with long red

Charly and I submerged ourselves in the revelry
of Mardi Gras. He was dressed as a cardinal and I
as a beggar maid. Swathed in ash-gray rags, tomato-
red corkscrew curls hanging around my chalk-white
face, I clung to him while he, in purple cloak and
cap with a large red cross on his breast, whispered
tenderly in my ear. We danced. We danced the
whole night through, carried along by jazz and
wine and we swayed and turned, weightless and
effortless, until dawn and hunger assailed us. We
had grown used to our masks and to the hundreds
of others around us: there were clowns and devils
and peasants, pirates and skeletons; Pierrots and
Eskimos; Cossacks, ghosts, pastry cooks, gardeners,
captains, sailors, generals, Jews, boxers, bathers, and
kings; fishermen, mermaids, dancing girls, gypsies,
poets, soldiers, and fakirs, and I don't know what
else. All of them had become familiar to us in the
course of the night, and each one was what he
seemed to be. Only with the coming of daylight and
hunger did the masks become untruthful, and many
of us now looked disheveled and embarrassed. Now
we were frightened of each other and hastened
home through the pale cold. There was scarcely a
taxi to be had. Charly had lost the cross off his

costume, and his biretta, and the beggar urchin slipped her freezing hand into his as I tripped along beside him through the crackling frost.

In front of us walked a stocky man with white knee socks who carried the mask of a fox or a coyote or a wolf in his hand. He kept turning his head to look at us in a way that seemed sinister to us. But finally we got a taxi after all; and as it hurried, sliding through the icy streets, we kept each other warm and did not give another thought to the little athlete with the coyote mask.

But there was something sinister going on, although those who never left home did not become aware of it, as one does not become aware of stale air in a room unless entering it from the freshness of outdoors. So, when we had been away—to Paris, for example, where I attended an art school, or far north at the seashore—and returned to our town, then we noticed that these "coyotes" were up to something here. I mean those stocky men with white knee socks and the malevolent glances.

At that time we had a house on the Baltic, situated far up in the Courland region. My father was born on the Baltic, and he was always drawn to it or to any other ocean. Beside the fact that most

young people are usually enchanted by the sea, it
was in our blood, and we were all happy there.

The house lay in the middle of a pine wood, a
quarter of an hour's walk from the beach. It had
brown wooden walls, blue shutters, and a thatched
roof, and it looked out on the inlet, the so-called
"shallows." We were cared for by a local girl whose
sturdy body and blond pigtail made her look like a
Caucasian peasant. Barefooted, in a long, heavy
skirt, she would stride through the wind, and when
the air caught at her skirt and blew it upward her
broad, red face grew a little broader and a little
redder as she jubilantly cried, "The sin of it! The
sin!"

It is astonishing how the sea can remove us from
time and events, how there is something comforting
and purifying about it. Its cleansing power affects
not only our bodies, but our souls as well.

We roamed through the near-endless dunes of fine
white sand and through the limitless pine woods
where the salt wind rustled and where an animal
sometimes appeared suddenly between the trees,
seemingly transfixed in reverie. Staglike, and yet not
a stag, for it was more powerful, with enormous ant-
lers, it stood between the trunks as if rooted, another

of its kind behind it, a second and a third to one side:
a whole frozen herd of these majestic antlered crea-
tures that were called elks. They let us approach
quite near without moving or altering their gently
fixed look. They were presumably unafraid, because
they were regarded as a kind of good omen in the
district and were not hunted. Only when we were
close enough to touch them would they turn and
stampede away, so that the forest floor groaned and
trembled.

And we roamed along the endless beach and ca-
vorted among the waves, and in the evenings we
strolled under the stars which nowhere but at the
shore are so bright and clear and multitudinous. And
we let the sun and the wind darken our skin, and
watched the moon as it waned and then grew full,
carelessly letting each day follow the one before.
Once we set off fireworks, and the colored, hissing
rockets rose to the stars, while the fishermen and
their families watched with legs set wide and gaping
mouths.

Sometimes it would rain for days at a time; then
sea and sky were one. Dunes, woods, scattered
thatched-roofed houses, all dissolved into a damp
gray, an oddly powerful, "unsad" melancholy.

My father, who at that time was working on *Young Joseph,* seemed in good spirits; one could hardly tell from observing him that he was disturbed by the evil forebodings of the time. On the beach he liked to watch a tanned, well-built boy, who from morning to night practiced jumping and running, discus throwing and javelin throwing, walking on his hands while the small of his back curved inward, and turning cartwheels like a peacock. It was a joy to observe his pliable body. "Body Joy"—Papa's careless nickname for him—frequently came to our "citadel," where he played ball with us, wearing his maroon sweat pants and a beret, his chest bare. We liked him. But how easy it was to imagine "Body Joy" in high boots and a uniform and with—oh—a cat-o'-nine-tails in his belt, to be used for teaching Jews to walk on their hands. . . . In our simple, southern town, friendliness could no longer flourish. It was being undermined by perversion and power lust, boiling up into a storm.

A movement born of negation must arouse dread; one whose cornerstone is the lie must repel. With what eely smoothness did this movement come to power! By one man's appealing to the next and placing responsibility on him, and that one in turn leaning on the man behind him, a long unbreakable chain of lies was forged. A man who acts in the name of another—whether good or bad—is not a man in any case but, deprived of his own will and responsibility, an empty vessel: the horrifying aspect of the movement was its false virility. One could see certain men in the town squares and at the beer-hall tables swaggering, orating, bursting into threatening laughter, or conspiring in canny undertones. These were the malcontents (the cowards, the confused) who now, under the protection of an emblem worn in their buttonholes and free from all responsibility, wanted to seize power at any cost. We did not simply see these men at a distance and indistinctly; we could scent even in the person of a neighbor or a friend the hidden "conspirator," the one who intended to soar up to fantastic heights at the expense of others.

And when they had chosen to lead them that man who crowned and exemplified their false virility and their false ideals, then for us there was no remaining.

❀❀❀

Book Three

The mechanized Middle Ages had come on the scene; science and destruction, progress and sadism went hand in hand. The heart of our country was stretched on the rack. Those who had been small became big, the base rose to the top, the fettered thought themselves freed by the agency of force.

If when I began these memoirs I spoke about the earnest striving, the inward struggle, the Christian urge towards self-expression, I can say now that the "movement" in our country, with its devotion to externals, was antichristian. My father had not been the only one who had seen the evil grow and who had seized every opportunity to utter words of warning. Now that crime and folly had triumphed and reigned in the name of freedom, he turned away, outraged. He sat on the little verandah of his studio in the south of France and stared in horror ahead of him, blind to the glowing color of the flowers, to the blue of sea and sky.

He was not yet prepared to be a "world citizen"; he felt the loss of his home as the destruction of himself. And his utter impotence in the face of his countrymen's devastation paralyzed him. "Well?" his look seemed to say. "I am outside, but what is happening inside, where is it to lead? It's unthinkable." And his gaze grew dark as he seemed to repeat that despairing "Well?" It was useless sitting down to write. Joseph might stay in his cave and be torn to pieces by wild animals, and Jacob might weep. As it was, everything was cause for weeping.

Dispossession, loss of citizenship, the book burning, and all the other indignities and abuses inflicted on my father were only a particle of the whole, a tiny symptom of a ghastly derailment, an immense confusion, which was spreading like a fire driven before wind.

Since these horrors were being perpetrated in the name of an exalted nationalism, since the idea of nationalism was being so totally perverted, the outside world automatically reduced the importance of

❀❀❀

this idea to a minimum, preserving it only as a kind of private privilege. People were German, French, Dutch, British, Belgian in the most unobtrusive and humble way. Privately, or as a matter of psychological interest it might be interesting to determine "what" one was, but overtly it was no longer important. Under the influence of the general disintegration and the drift towards cosmopolitanism which were the order of the day, nationalism became ever more vague until it was dissolved into the universal. Joseph, the family baby and his father's darling, became a world citizen. Voluntarily or not, he overcame the hardships, wholly attained the new status, and was therefore destined for it. My father, too, surmounted the hardships and wholly attained the new and predestined status.

All of us—to a much smaller degree—were also destined to become children of the world; and just through this spiritual expansion did the words "family" and "home" gain new clarity and depth for us, since their "real" disappearance now made them purely inner concepts—a kind of secret treasure.

The exile wears his spiritual heritage like cleated shoes to keep him from slipping on the ice of foreign ground. My father spoke in French, drove a Peugeot

and ate croissants, but the "Goethe experience" remained strong within him, as did German *lieder* and
many other things. Inviolate things. True treasures
of the past, which could not be affected by today's
reality. Or could they be? One became cynical, sus-
pected relationships: Nietzsche, Wagner, Schiller,
Schumann . . . "unhealthy romanticism," "pomp"
and "hero worship": what retained its purity? But
wait! Pound the table with your fist! There was to
be no surrender; integrity must be maintained; it
was a duty, a man's duty.

Our first home in exile—or rather in self-banish-
ment, for the Nazis would have been only too glad
to win my father over, if only because they were
afraid to have him for an enemy—our first home in a
foreign country was called "La Tranquille."

Plays, concerts, and operas, lecture tours and receptions—the worldly things which had colored my
father's life in spite of his hard-working seclusion—
came to an end. Here it was quiet; after the initial
horror and depression had worn off, our senses and
feelings unfolded before the manifold attractions of
the south. The bittersweet splendor of the scene
began to uplift our souls and invigorate our spirits.
My father took up his work again, and our life re-

❀❀❀

sumed a comparatively normal aspect. It was as if
we were establishing ourselves in vagueness, never
knowing what might be the duration of the horror,
or its effect on our own fates and on the world's
destiny. This condition of apprehensive tension
made it more necessary than ever for us to engage
in some sort of activity, and awakened in us a great
yearning for the positive. We seized every good
thing as if it were a gift—the beauty of the landscape, friends, the picturesquenesss of the old fishing
harbor, and finally the sea. . . . All in all, "out
here" we seemed more open to impressions, more receptive to and more sensible of true values, and "La
Tranquille," in spite of all that was dark in the background, became a place for work, for affectionate
meetings, and for contemplation.

❀❀❀

[II]

Our numbers were steadily increasing. The places where freedom still prevailed attracted more and more people who lived where there was none. Terror swept over Europe like a passion, and soon there was no place at all for us. We flooded Switzerland and were glad and grateful that this was allowed us. But our flood could not stop the terrifying bonfire whose flames threatened to leap the frontier at any moment. There was a smell of world-wide explosion in the air.

At the outbreak of war, my parents found themselves on an America-bound Dutch liner, full to the bursting point. America: for me at first it was only a word—and yet there was something very distant and abstract about it that inspired me with a kind of easy respect, curiosity, and a quiet dread. Perhaps this was only because it was so far away, and also because in my imagination that monotony of freedom, equality, and happiness was reduced to the eccentricity of its people and of its nature, to skyscrapers, hurricanes, vast prairies, and neon advertisements which seemed to represent life on another planet.

When we first came to America my father held an honorary professorship at Princeton and lived in a house which, when I got to know it later, reminded me a little of a haunted castle with its overgrown garden, weathered walls, creaking stairs, and the large high-backed chairs covered with red damask in dimly lit rooms which should really have been guarded by a sinister-looking lackey. Instead there was chocolate-colored John in the white jacket, who knew how to offer his services to "Mr. and Mrs. Man" with a cheerily flashing grin. Sometimes John was absent from his duties because, as his wife—who looked after the kitchen—explained, he was in bed and "disgusted." John had a great deal of imagination and a kind heart, and for that reason he was presumably easily "disgusted" by the unhappy circumstances of his race. Once John explained to me,

❀❀❀

with a winning child-like smile, the problem of the "Black Sheep" by saying, "There is no black God, there is no white God, but there is only one God." But at that moment the world seemed deserted by all the gods. . . .

At that time I was with my husband in London where the blitz was raging. Two years later I landed in the United States, a widow. The reddish, rock-bound coast of the south of France with its prickly, colorful vegetation, its dusty vine-covered hills, its bold speech, its then antediluvian motor coaches, its Sanary, Toulon, and Marseilles which, like all port towns, are penetrated with a kind of operatic bravado—this world I exchanged first for exemplary and courteous Switzerland.

After that I went to Florence, with which and in which I fell in love, and Vienna, which preceded London in my European farewell. In Florence, which now leaves me cold, I grew enthusiastic about the harmonious intermingling of solemn and simple, of Renaissance pomp and dark, odorous little streets which led directly into the country. Between the city and the surrounding country there seemed a living bond. The ancient walls, towers, and cupolas lay nestled between the vineyards and the cypress-covered hills, and the evening sky sometimes spread a violet light over all. The Tuscan landscape is the most peaceful one I know, despite its antiphony of gloom and beauty. It is a poetic landscape, and there is poetry, too, in its capital, Florence.

At that time the city seethed with life. Hardly touched by Fascism, it had become a small international enclave of elegance and culture, enjoyed by those who found refuge in its gracefulness and ingenuousness. Florence was aware of its qualities. It was fastidious and arrogant; those who wanted to live there had to qualify somehow. I consider my sojourn there a distinction and reward.

Today it has become a tourist center without individuality, a stage setting, in which a genuine light glows only rarely.

Then I lived right among those odoriferous little streets, where fish and incense and cats and coffee and olive oil and cheese and sun and jostling crowds blended into an artless and precious whole. I lived in a half-ruined tower, at the top of a hundred and twenty-three steps, where I practiced the piano tirelessly and held receptions. To the studio came young art historians, doctors, musicians, painters, philosophers, and ne'er-do-wells—all those who didn't shy

❀❀❀

away from the steps leading to the half-ruined roof terrace with its magnificent view—and there was wine punch, laughter, dancing, and conversation about art.

In the early summer mornings I went to the Piazza Michel Angelo, gathered figs and flowering branches, and watched the passing monks and street cleaners, while the city itself bathed in golden sunshine. I visited the museums and gardens, and, in the evenings, the cloisters of San Domenico. I attended concerts and salons where young Florentine artists and old aristocratic British ladies sat beside open fires and listened to chamber music over bottles of old wine.

I was alone for weeks at a time, observing the life in the streets and churches, and keeping myself busy in my plain studio. In winter a little old woman brought brushwood and logs to my tower and taught me the indispensable art of lighting the stove. I was astonished at the crone's nimbleness when she caught a mouse dancing among the pedals while I was playing a Schumann "Phantasie."

Because the city was so beautiful and so stimulating, it was easy to be alone in it. One could dream there. And I dreamed of a stranger—at least of a man I had met only once. And the more I dreamed of him, the more I understood that he wasn't a stranger at all. There was so much in him that I knew, only too well, and anything that was strange gave impetus to my dreams. Dreams need room for what is not yet, for what might be. This "might be" exists even in reality, whose solid, definable colors are lit by it to an iridescent, pearly glow. No existence is so tangible that it simply "is." Fear and longing part to reveal a glimpse of the other, to transform the known existence into the unknown, the longed-for, and the feared. The uncertainty, the danger of this being enhance its value; it is born of a kind of dreamy pride or reverent conceit that attributes deep meanings and relationships to one's own fate, yet paradoxically it is born too of a humility as deep as the presumption. If you form an attachment which you feel is preordained, you are placing it in the realm of the supra- or super-natural, in spheres that are hardly your domain—and yet the very spheres where lie our presentiments and beliefs, the "creative" and the religious.

The familiar stranger of whom I had dreamed became mine. From the beginning there was a reverent pride in this relationship which gave it deep significance and weighted it with presentiments. That iridescent, unsteady element, in which dark lights played, glowed only briefly and disappeared like a rainbow, and for the rest it was a genuine, healthy and happy union.

We moved between Florence, Zurich, and Vienna, until we went to London, planning to travel to the United States by way of Canada.

What would be the meaning of that bond of common interests in literature and music and nature, the similar outlook on life, without that all-and-nothing that unites two people, without the mutual giving, the receptivity of one to the other—without that pollen of the soul that intermingles? To be sure, in tangible matters they will always remain two, and their unity is only spiritual.

I was proud of my attachment to a man of enthusiasms—for he was enthusiastic, through and through. He suffered for his ideals and principles as though they burned within him, and gave them a seemingly cosmic importance. Yet he could, in turn, look on them with humor.

Peculiar to him was the oriental languor and contemplativeness of his being, which was allied with a classicism, an almost fanatic drive toward clarity,

❀❀❀

"authenticity," and integrity. He was constantly
fighting for the recognition and preservation of these
things. Confusion, half-heartedness, and compromise inspired him with honest anger. Much as he
liked to laugh, much as he enjoyed humor, it was
impossible to joke with him: then his natural amia-
bility was transformed into harshness and inexora-
bility, filling the air like a pungent oath. Since life
often required compromises, life was not easy for
him. He often felt himself to be an "outsider," solitary, and he accepted all the more gratefully such
conviviality and friendship as were offered him. He
had not chosen his profession accidentally, for in it
he felt that he was able to demonstrate the true and
the genuine; he seemed born for that meshing of art
and scholarship that characterizes the task of the art
historian.

Sculpture—probably the most accessible of all art
forms, since it is the most palpable and direct—was
the object of his researches, which he undertook
with pedantic vehemence, intuitive logic, knowl-
edgeable guesswork, mathematical perception, and
controlled passion—combining within himself the
qualities of the poet and scientist. The results must
have been outstanding and impressive, since he was

❀❀❀

known among his colleagues as a scholar with revolutionary, revelatory methods and ideas. His love
and energy were mainly devoted to the work of
Donatello, whom he penetrated, as it were, to the
marrow and discovered anew for us. I am not a
devotee of the fine arts, and I was a weak pupil of
my husband's who could follow his efforts only in a
very narrow way. But it was impossible not to trust
them, not to believe in his discoveries, not to recognize his results—he could convince the layman or the
child with such a clean passion: rather as an orchestra conductor might convince a deaf man. . . .

Italy held him for years, especially Florence,
where he shone as a connoisseur of façades and an
authority on the Catacombs. He would climb up
rickety scaffolding under the cupola in the cathedral
to dust off some tiny bronze angel and examine it
microscopically. One would see him in the most un-
likely places, trying to keep his balance, either alone
or with artisans and assistants: high up on Gatte-
malata's horse in Padua, on the bosom of the cruel
Judith in front of the Palazzo Vecchio, on the beard
of an evangelist on one of the pillars of the Baptistry
in Florence. . . .

These art historians, religious chroniclers, and

archeologists are pure adventurers. Like the mountaineer on the Himalayas or the explorer at the North Pole who do not hesitate to probe and triumph over the extremes of nature, the dignified, gray-bearded professor is not afraid to spend weeks digging under the hot sun in the rubbish of Greece, or crawling about in the cold ruins of Etruscan graves, in the hope of "getting at time's origins."

✾✾✾

In Vienna too there were already many stocky men with white knee socks and threatening looks, so we didn't stay there long. On the wings of power they darkened the sky like a plague of locusts. We just managed to see casually magnificent Vienna with its parks and palaces and wine-steeped suburbs, its smart urbanity and deep-rooted love of art. We passed through the Salzkammergut, its mountains, forests, and lakes, where there was so much rain and so many "Marterl"—those little wayside shrines holding primitive holy pictures which cling to the trees like birds' nests. The air was redolent with the scent of berries, mushrooms, resin, and Mozart.

After that we dawdled a while in the old town of Zurich—where the bells ring far too noisily, but whose austere antiquity is appetizing, and whose narrow "mewses" with their bakers', grocers' and handicraft shops, we could more easily imagine peopled by characters out of Gottfried Keller than by the drunken louts we encountered.

In London we occupied ourselves with art history and music and took leave of Europe and—without knowing it—of each other.

This metropolis is made for gloomy thoughts, and in truth the happy mood in our apartment overlooking Kensington Gardens was darkened by pathetic forebodings. The great disaster, which not only involved us but affected us personally, broke out. The sky over London was encircled by a net of balloons in which the locusts were meant to entangle themselves should they appear. They might appear at any moment. They did appear. My most vivid memory of that period—to which one became accustomed as to any period—is the equanimity of that darkly monumental city—now outwardly it was transformed into a hell and inwardly preserved an inviolate dignity. It met the noise, the tension, the deprivation, and the devastation with such decorum as probably only the English can muster. Alive in my memory are the sirens which overwhelmed us while

❀❀❀

we were sleeping, cooking, making music, or strolling in Hyde Park among magnificent flowers and trees —the sirens that roused us like the trump of Judgment, the sirens that heralded the satanic squadrons; the blackout, which seemed like a macabre game of hide-and-seek and which gave London on a moonlit night an unforgettable beauty; the gas masks, which we slung around our shoulders as if they were the most ordinary thing in the world—opera glasses, or a shopping bag.

Yes, at bottom we grew to accept all of it as a matter of course; in the midst of the horror we went out to work and even in pursuit of pleasure. Even if we should suddenly be seized by a great shudder, a great protest stifled by the unalterability of events. Yes, under our composure there was a protest like a flame, pale in the glare of those other immense, scorching flames, but undying.

Although we had chosen London only as a gateway to the United States, we still felt a little like deserters when we had our Canadian visas in our pockets. And—in spite of all the horrors—London had grown dear to us: the boundless city which wore its gray, shabby dress as if it were a king's mantle; whose Westminster bells (then stilled) were a boom-

❀❀❀

ing, echoing symbol of a great, ended history; whose people seemed to draw their humor and their philosophy from the fog itself; London, a city at once so gloomy and so festive—yes, a festive finale, the last oasis of European civilization. While we were sharing so fully in this experience, we often looked at each other with sad smiles and turned away. On the train to Liverpool we waved at a young couple—a girl and a boy in British uniform. It seemed that we were not really leaving them, that their fate was also ours.

For many years, day and night, I was troubled by the nightmarish reality, experienced in every fiber and yet so totally improbable, of that wartime adventure that so immediately followed our departure with its many hopes and just as many dark premonitions, and in which my husband lost his life. Everything happened within a quarter of an hour. The explosion, the discipline in the beginning, the panic, the deep plunge, chaos on the burning ship, our calling out, our sinking into silence . . . but in its immeasurable terribleness the event took on the dimension of eternity—of untimeliness, happening in its own despite, backwards, not at all, underneath

❀❀❀

us. And, although it was happening with inexorable sharpness, far from being more readily comprehensible it was because of this more negative and horrifying, having no connection with us—yet we were it, we were made of horror and transgression. So the extremes of actuality can be totally abstract: looking at it soberly, this is gladdening, since the abstract reaches the divine. Will you believe me that the divine was operating even here? While I drifted for twenty hours in the stormy fall waters of the Atlantic on a piece of wood, being and nothingness mingled, as did down and up, dark and light, end and beginning, curse and blessing, abandonment and the nearness of God. An English battleship brought me to Scotland to a hospital. There was a ward there for the feeble-minded, and I will never forget the visits of an idiot who strewed gifts on the counterpanes of those of us who had been shipwrecked—oranges, chocolates. . . .

I told my sister all that had happened to me. There had been a kind of lurch, as if we had struck something. Bells sounded the alarm. Yes, it was at night, about half past ten. I had already fallen asleep, and he came down from the lounge where he had been

playing the piano—Bach's "Well Tempered Clavi-
chord"—when the bells sounded he came to the
cabin, pale; first he adjusted my life belt, then his
own. What we were wearing? Only raincoats. We
took nothing with us, there wasn't time. We were in
lifeboat number six; there were far too many people
in it, far more than could fit, because there was a
scarcity of lifeboats—some had been destroyed by
the torpedo—and we all fell nearly to the bottom of
the sea because there were too many of us and because the ropes were rotten. There was a lot of crazy
noise from the crew, black men, they just yelled.
And when we rose to the surface again we yelled
too, as well as we could. We had swallowed oil and
were exhausted and sought something we could
cling to, and as we called to each other I heard his
call, three times, and then nothing more. And then
I was surrounded by corpses, and by deep black
night and high waves, and I was thirsty, and my
voice was gone, and my hands were infinitely cold,
and once I vomited and soiled my scarf—my green-
and-brown-checked wool scarf, his last birthday present to me, which was later taken by a sailor on the
English battleship. The waves hurled themselves on

me like huge, black mountains. There were dead children, killed by shock and cold and thirst—oh, that thirst!—and they floated like dolls. It rained in torrents, then the moon came out, now the dead children floated on the waves in the moonlight. A married couple had died, a man with a heavy beard and a stout little woman who had always been so comfortable that even now, in death, they seemed comfortable still. The man cradled the woman's head carefully in his lap, and he wore the same hat he had always worn on the ship, where his cigar had never been out of his mouth—I think he did not know that his little wife was dead in his lap—and all at once he gave a cozy puff and blow, as if he were blowing out his beloved cigar smoke—but it was his death gasp, and at the same instant his head rolled awry. . . .

My sister could not understand how I had endured all· this; she thought it miraculous. I indicated my hands, as if they could explain it. I just held on tight, so tight. To the raft or the piece of wood, to the shred of ship? Yes. To life, you probably held on to life, my sister may have thought. And the next afternoon at four o'clock the English battleship came—and that took us back to Scotland where I

❀❀❀

am now, so full of that miracle, and so empty. . . .

Tears choke me. The thousand details, all the confusion centers around the one person, around him who had ceased to be. His name was Jenoe Lányi.

❀❀❀

[IV]

The noise and glitter of New York were shattering
and intimidating. I sat silent beside my mother in
the car. John at the wheel half turned and indicated
the Empire State building. I saw that in the flick-
ering half-light a secret-proud smile crossed his
face. "That's how things are here, Miss Moni, it
startles you, doesn't it?" he seemed to say. I must
have replied with an "Oh," or "Ah," or "Uhu" in
my surprise, and my syllables sounded more sincere
when we drove along the Hudson past the glittering
skyline.

From New York to Princeton was about an hour's
drive on a smooth, broad highway, shining with a
constant stream of cars. As they glided along there
seemed to be no people in them, and the skyscrapers

108

too seemed uninhabited. It was a lifeless picture. It was soothing. At least it silenced my soul, which had been much too loud. America's abundance and exuberance, glitter, noise, wealth, careless prodigality—this so-called happiness struck me at first as so ironic that it numbed me. The jazz, the football, the revelry of the advertisements, the pace that seemed constantly to be saying: "On, forward, don't stop, don't think, don't become aware of life, rise above it with cars and machines and movies and radios and airplanes. Don't pause, or the scruples will set in and the doubts. Forward!" And these unscrupulous currents numbed me at first.

Was I homesick for the dark, for the black ocean hills, did I want to return to the no-man's land between being and nothingness, between curse and blessing, between alienation and God's nearness, did I desire the doubts, the fears, the hope and longing? The answer to these questions began as a feeling of helpless defeat which gradually dissolved. By and by I was no longer dazzled and numbed by the purely colossal; I abstracted from it, as it were, its component parts, and slowly it assumed warmth, personality, a soul. There were, for example, the brightly glowing autumn foliage of Princeton; and

❀❀❀

Roosevelt's voice; and our friend Molly, and Roggers who played Beethoven and Schubert, whose music stood out even in the damask hall of the American "haunted castle."

Europe was not a lost or abandoned continent here, but a related one. As the new world grew more familiar I made an effort to connect it with the old, so that the one might support and supplement the other. Here as everywhere else security grew around one, and one could adapt without compromising oneself. One drifted with the stream, because one neither could nor wanted to go against it. My British accent changed, before I knew it, to a sturdy American speech, to that most optimistic of all ways of speech. Where else would you be called "honey" with so much undisguised elation and confidence, and where else would you say "Okay" with so much intoxicated assurance? And I grew used to the sight of the moon which, with equally intoxicated assurance, hung crookedly against the sky in that hemisphere; and to the drugstore where, after you had weathered the first shock, a kind of functional coziness reigned, where you could shop for anything from a toothbrush to a radio, where you could have a splinter in your eye attended to and where you

❁❁❁

could get breakfast, where in spite of the unidentifiable odors the excellence of a milk shake could be genuinely enjoyed, and where the mechanical sobriety, the blank assembly-line activity, had an almost cheering effect.

Yes, I was cheered by this functional, hygienic, practical atmosphere, not only because it made life easier, but also because these gleaming machines, buttons, and fixtures—as they independently accomplished complicated procedures, squeezed oranges, made coffee and "shakes," washed dishes, cleaned carpets, scrubbed windows, opened cans, sliced hams, and peeled potatoes—had something magic in their clever cunning and suggested the amusing concept that we humans were a luxury and that they, the bright little machines, could get along without us very well. Even the skyscrapers and the cars that frightened me at first now seemed to me gay; since they were a manifestation of the masses but not of the individual, they elevated the single human being to the position of a rarity, a delicacy, and it is true that in this country a human relationship is more highly valued than anywhere else.

[V]

". . . She looked up at the sky and wondered where her son's soul had gone. Was it following her, or was it suspended among the stars and no longer thinking of her? Oh, how lonely it is in the fields at night, surrounded by song when you cannot sing yourself, surrounded by uninterrupted cries of joy when there is no happiness for you, when the sky reflects the equally lonely moon who is indifferent." (Anton Chekhov.)

I call to that young mother: "The soul of your child is in you and you are in it; but all the same the earth has become lonely, under the unfeeling sky." Who has not felt the indifference of the sky, which spreads day-and-night over our events as if nothing at all were happening? But if it could show sym-

❀❀❀

pathy, what would remain for us? Is it not this very indifference that kindles our own feelings? When lightning strikes a majestic tree, or hail destroys the young shoots and blossoms, is it not the very absurdity of it that shocks and moves us? Are we not touched by the abyss that yawns between the infinitely unfeeling universe and our own limited sensitivity? Nevertheless, we must trust chance whenever a bridge seems to span the gulf. Blind fate appears more meaningful, more human, and we ourselves seem to expand until somewhere, somehow we find a common meeting place. . . .

I look up at the sky, and wonder where my father's soul has gone. . . . It is lonely. I lie under a tree that has been blasted by lightning. No leaf, no branch. Half charred, half split. The rotting yellow wood is full of beetles. I think I hear a knocking in the lifeless trunk. But everything is silent. I begin to dream, and recognize the rich green leaves and the pale blossoms, and experience the wonderful intoxicating scent. I realize that I am not dreaming but remembering, that what I see and recognize is not illusion and fantasy, but reality which the lightning has transformed into a different truth. It is thus that I remember my father—fragmentary images,

❀❀❀

isolated happenings and thoughts come to me here, things seemingly transitory in the light of eternity.

There—or not? Ah, yes, the floor creaks, there are steps on the stairs, doors are opened and shut: he has walked through. And? But is this nothing? He has passed through the house. The floors, the brown wooden staircase with the Persian runner, the softly tinted, gold-framed etchings of Joseph on the staircase walls hold his presence for a little while. Strange, isn't it? When one of us passes through, this does not happen. Was it because his step was loud and echoing, because he was humming to himself, or was there anything strange about his passing? No, nothing at all.

His step was light and regular, he did not hum, he walked neither quickly nor slowly. He glanced in passing at the mail on the piano, where letters he had written were still lying unstamped in a tidy pile, perhaps eight of them, their tedious addresses carefully printed in neat Spencerian letters, the names of the towns underlined with a sure, slightly upward stroke. Mielein would attend to them later. My father had left his glasses on his desk. His expression was not tense or excited, but cheerful and ordinary: "Okay." He went into his bedroom and

❀❀❀

shut the door behind him, neither loudly nor quietly. Really nothing remarkable, absolutely not. And yet I can only declare that the house was full of his presence for quite a while.

It is evening: the cigar is lit, there is Turkish coffee which he has made himself. He pats the poodle, saying "Good boy." The poodle grins, sits up on his hind legs, and with his round golden eyes looks straight into my father's blue ones. What does the little fool want, what's the dog after, why is he looking at me like that? The poodle grins, and with his elegant, carefully tended claws scratches at my father's hand, so that it gets quite red. Then my father brings out a red object which was once a ball, but which because of the dog's affection is now quite unrecognizable. That's what the doggy wants, is it? My father throws it up; the poodle jumps from his begging position as if there were a spring inside his body, and catches the flying ball in his mouth. The animal is so amused and gratified at his own trick that his heart jumps for joy. There he sits now with the red blob in his mouth, his sides heaving, his eyes shining with the joy of the game. Again? Once more? All right, once more. . . .

And now the record player is going. My father

is looking up, his mouth slightly open, his head turned back a little as if he were sleeping with open eyes, almost as if he were dead. Hardly have the last notes sounded than he says something—something or other about the final chorus of *Fidelio*. His words caress the music, like the touch of a hand on something living. So he has not been asleep—not a bit of it; he has given himself up to the music, wide awake, unafraid, like one who has dived under water and holds his breath, unconscious of himself. Surely one might die this way. But he touched the music with his words, as if it were a being with features and senses that stood before him, always offering something new, no matter how well he already knew it.

Then he retires to his "dais," the small platform at the back window in the study. The study is not very big, but now he seems very far away. I don't know why. He sits under a reading lamp, a small rug under his feet, smokes his cigar, and reads. "Good night!" We hear and marvel at his far-away contentment—it was as if a man were sitting on Venus, smoking a cigar and browsing among old books. We leave the room and shut the door behind us, still wondering.

❀❀❀

It's only when we are halfway up the stairs that we begin to whistle and cease to wonder.

Nonexistence as such is unimaginable. It only emerges when opposed to existence; only then does it take on life; only in the face of what is given do we comprehend what is taken. And while I look at the sea or eat a meal or laugh at a comedian, suddenly I am aware that my father does not see the ocean, does not taste the meal, does not laugh at the clown, and only then do I recognize his not-being. This knowledge struck me with the deepest, saddest clarity the other day while I was listening to a Mozart quartet. The fact that he was not hearing this made me suddenly and overwhelmingly conscious of his nothingness. The feeling was so strong that it lasted only a moment. I tried to explore it, penetrate it, but it fled. An electrifying knowledge and mourning had seized me and fled, escaped into the dark like a demon.

Hearing is a peculiar sense—it can lay bare a world like a flash of lightning.

Both my nephews were born in California but went to school in Switzerland, and in their polite

German there is an echo of many Swiss intonations
—and why not? They often visit at my parents' home,
where they enjoy the love of their grandparents, the
excellent meals, and most of all the grand jokes and
stories of Grandpapa. They are at dinner with us—
enlivened by roast chicken and chocolate pudding
—and the smaller one, who is seldom in a mood to
talk tells an anecdote about his school. In the
course of the story he uses the word "Mädchen,"
which he speaks with that open, drawn-out, slightly
lilting "ä" of the Swiss, and it sounds comical and
touching. It sounds gracious, and old-fashioned and
innocent and surprising—perhaps all of us notice it.
I see that my father is infinitely moved by it. As the
sound strikes his ear, his gaze sweeps over the little
boy with a smile that is full of tender melancholy;
he seems steeped in a deep and smiling compassion
for the child-as-such in his gracefulness, his help-
lessness, his enigmatic being. And all because of the
sound which had fallen so unintentionally from the
lips of this hearty little boy.

My father goes for a walk in the rain. There are
many people in the street. There is no mistaking him.
He is the epitome of a man walking in the rain. Not
as if he were propagandizing rain, like that flawless,

waterproofed man in the newspaper, with his broad shoulders, narrow hips, overcoat, shining galoshes, and pipe, suffering the cloudburst under the water-proofed hat, his angular face devoid of any expression, of whom one cannot for a moment believe that he has any connection with the forces of nature or that the downpour could even sprinkle him. My father was not like that.

He wears an old trench coat and a hat, ordinary shoes, and walks along, holding aloft an open umbrella, totally adapted to the situation—almost as if the situation had adapted itself to him. He seems to absorb the situation with composure and humility. The crease in his gray-flannel trousers is almost gone and several clots of mud cling to them. He wants to cross the street—a car approaches on the left, still pretty far away. He stands still, umbrella in hand, and waits. The rain pelts down on his umbrella, the car has gone splashing by. He crosses the street with long strides, holding the umbrella unusually high. Arrived on the far sidewalk, he brushes his chest as if to remove dust. Then he walks on at his usual pace. He inclines the umbrella a little against one shoulder because the wind is at his back, and looks ahead, until suddenly the wind snatches his um-

❁❁❁

brella. For a moment he holds it in front of him like
a shield, as it drags him along in all directions, so
that he describes a circle around himself—always
careful to hold the umbrella against the wind. Now
the wind turns the umbrella inside out, bends it back,
then turns it right side out again. Finally he holds
the rescued umbrella over his head. His blue, meek
glance is suddenly filled with weariness, his nose
emerges more sharply from between his eyes, his
narrow, clean-shaven face has aged, seems to trem-
ble a little. Shadowed by the umbrella, it expresses
a sense of the tragic from which it is slowly freed as
he goes on walking, step by step, in the rain that has
become gentle and steady, until at last in this over-
cast monotony his face takes on a friendly glow.
Around the long upper lip and the graying, short
mustache plays a suggestion of a youthful smile.

He sings. Hamming a song by Schubert, Brahms,
Strauss or Wolf—with chin and eyebrows slightly
raised, eyes glowing with delicious recognition. I
said, he hams—he does not sing in the technical
sense—and yet his singing is complete. (No professional musician sings like that—how badly they often
sing, and God knows why! They shriek and wail to
demonstrate a lyrical passage, and treat their voice

❀❀❀

as if it were a freak.) And he does not sing like a dilettante; he sings as he alone can. He forms the melody and sketches acoustically its development. One perceives its origin, its truth, and becomes a happy though slightly scandalized witness to such a rendering—at the lunch table, strolling in the garden, in the living room, *à propos de rien.*

A quarrel, harsh words—what in English is called "some argument"—with him are unthinkable. Is it because gentleness and arrogance make him tower over it all? Does he refuse to lower himself to an "argument"? Or is it because he does not take life's questions seriously, doesn't consider it worthwhile to get excited about them, thinks it doesn't pay to enter into deep dispute with another person, to stand fast, to persist, to assert a belief? That it doesn't seem worth it—is that because of indifference, "lukewarmness" such as Christ proscribed?

In spite of all his experience, in spite of all his reflection, he *knows* nothing. For knowledge is not a permanent thing, but something to be caught in the depths of the moment. He does not have it handy, like his opponent, and for the time being cannot counter with anything except ignorance, which his opponent takes for contempt. Even when he reaches

❀❀❀

into these depths and comes to a conclusion, it is still shifting and amorphous, verging on irony. For true irony is just such shifting knowledge: sliding, movable, living knowledge, as opposed to fixed, dead, formulated knowledge. Faced with this irony, it is easy to see one's own laboriously constructed judgment and belief grow foggy, lured into the immeasurable and dangerous realms of intuition. Even moral values are apt to dissolve in those pure and lawless regions—for ethics are not axiomatic, fixed, dead, but move and live in a wonderful and fearful way. With all his genuine aversion to evil, my father is not ready with judgment and condemnation, he looks beneath the surface of sin, which reveals to him its multifaceted loveliness and even a profound inner justification. A vagabond, a confidence man, or even one who commits incest may be a gleaming and glowing embodiment of sin. And if my father seems to be playing with evil, to flirt with it, it is because of his ironic, undefined knowledge of it, which is chiefly suffering. For there is no firm ground, and who can safeguard himself from The Fall?

By the way, the clearly logical, mathematical mode of thought is alien to him. It entertains him in a distant way, and forces an embarrassed smile

❀❀❀

from him. A brain that does lightning calculations, combines and speculates on numbers—such abstract skill is astonishing to the point of uncanniness. In the sphere of the intellect logic is necessary—no reasoning without logic—but logic as an end in itself, in its cold, crystal bareness, emits a soulless magic.

Mopping his forehead with a handkerchief scented with violet water—this is something I recognize: that forehead that expresses so much. It can be gay or solemn, calm or searching, but always—still unwrinkled even in old age—always it is clear and tolerant. He mops it with a kind of tender matter-of-factness, careful seriousness; the handkerchief retains its folds and returns neatly to its pocket. That handkerchief! Snowy white, scented, unfolded and used—the frequent gesture is like a paternal rite. Others make this gesture awkwardly, in clumsy haste, but he consummates it with full significance, as it were, though with "esthetic distance."

The esthete. Never give in to ineptness! And never let your feelings come to full expression; it might be too revealing, unesthetic. Feeling comes from him like a strong, invisible element; when he is cold he does not go "brr" and shiver—but it grows cold all around him. He makes himself understood with ele-

❀❀❀

mental force, with esthetic remoteness. The esthete. And nature, matter? How common, how cruel! Gloomy revulsion rises sky-high in him—he transcends the material, he inhabits the world of the spirit. He estheticizes his earthly weight. But in order to beautify something, to make it palatable, isn't it necessary to appreciate it—or to love it? It probably leads to this, that he loves the world and all that it contains—even those parts of it that hurt or frighten him. Love is the basis of his duality—love and ironic knowledge of the great unity and the inseparable wholeness of all being, of the divine interaction of all opposites. For that reason his life is strong, his death is strong; that is why death was implicit in his life, why life is implicit in his death.

Shimmering brightness fills the air. In this light I recognize his brow, which he mops with the violet-scented handkerchief after a summer midday walk— the serene and patient brow which discloses so much. Not a "thinker's brow," high, rounded and shiny, with the portentous hairline, but a human brow. A very human brow.

I tell him something. Something unimportant. I can feel how he makes the tale his own, imbues it with his personality, and how it comes back to me with changed meaning. My parents have moved into a new house—one of how many?—and I am visiting them. I don't yet know the district well, and when I go for a walk, I lose my way. I keep seeing the house, always from new perspectives, but I can't get to it. At last, hot and a little out of breath, I arrive in the dining room, where the family has almost finished dinner. I tell them, "I lost my way, kept seeing the house, and couldn't reach it. A herd of beautiful red-brown deer had been standing at the edge of the wood. . . ."

He smiles, and I see my casual words take on a kind of symbolic magic—the beckoning house, elusive under the scorching midday sun, the enchanted animals at the forest's edge gazing motionless in the direction of the searching mortal who has lost her way. . . .

Perhaps I tell him, "I know a blind cat, it lives in the small yellow barn." He listens, his brows drawn together, his head falling back a little, with the almost exaggerated astonishment and interest that one likes to show to children, and yet he is serious. He immediately grasps with all his being the oddity, the tragedy of the blind animal. How it cowers there, its watery, green eyes with their over-large black

❀❀❀

[VI]

In writing these memoirs I am trying to follow an orderly sequence. Not only may the mood change unintentionally, but recent happenings may displace those that preceded them. My father's death is still too much with me for me to want to tell much about him. One thing only: his presence was overwhelming. His absence is overwhelming. But his absence is full of presence, and was his presence not largely made up of absence? His being and not-being are wonderfully joined. Where else but in him were "the essence" and the public man combined so harmoniously? In whom else are a deep worldliness and modesty and electedness so paired, so organic as in him? It is true that many aspects meet in the great man. Contraries combine in him. It may be that

127

greatness requires the fusion of opposites—up-down, good-bad, harsh-mild, pain-joy, gravity-playfulness, beauty-ugliness, beginning-end, day-night, death-life. . . .

So it was not mere chance that my father's death coincided with the height of his success. Shortly before his end, on his eightieth birthday (it was said that no mortal had ever had such a celebration) he said, with a happy, rueful smile, "I have a feeling that my life is dissolving in celebration," and added, humorously reassuring us, "I hope it will all calm down once more." So this celebration of life was dedicated to death. Strange—I had just written the words "haunted castle" (using it ironically) when I was forced to break off.

I will say this, that the contrasting elements of Europe and America blend well together. It is quite wrong to suppose that to acclimatize oneself to the new one must discard the old, be ashamed of it, deny it. It is more honest devoutly to preserve the one and marry it to the other. The new customs and rules and conditions merge effortlessly with old habits, as new sounds ally themselves to the ground bass.

❀❀❀

Past & Present

The Princeton palace with its shadowy rooms and enchanted thorn gardens, its dinners for American professors and the gracious, protective care of its Negro servants was a transposition of yesterday into the exotic present; there we were, truly ourselves, yet moved to another world. The self of the past, bound and weighted with memories and traditions, became more a part of that grandiose, free, light atmosphere; and although ethically and geographically we were so far from home, we felt here for the first time the oneness of the whole world.

Paradoxically, this was even more apparent after the United States entered the war. Indeed, the more comprehensive the carnage and the greater the struggle between the nations, the more clearly we sensed the inescapable unity of the world now manifesting itself so tragically. All suffered, all were involved, all condoned the frightful means toward an end without significance in the dark night of universal pain. The fact that my brothers fought against their native land, that my own country had robbed me of my husband—even this was an indication of the inescapable brotherhood of man. The tragic devastation and dispersion of the nations must end in their harmonious integration.

❁❁❁

After three years at Princeton my parents moved
to California, where they considered the climate
more suitable. True, when they lived in the timeless
West, they may have longed for changing seasons,
clouds, and storms. May have longed for Princeton,
for example, when its attractive, treelined streets lay
in the cold austerity of winter; when Christmas trees
shone jewellike from snow-covered doorways at
night; when Papa went for a walk at noon on the
shoveled paths, and was amused at the poodle, Niko,
rolling in the snow like a ball of black wool. . . .
These days were no more.

Now they were removed from time and space,
further from reality but closer to truth. In the endless light, the unending expanse of sea and desert
and human unscrupulousness, the awul truth of
world events was clearly visible. One felt caught up
in the crisis, and in some way responsible for it, so
that my father continually interrupted his work on
the Joseph series to instruct and warn his erring
brethren. Not only did he once or twice a week
travel many miles from his home in Pacific Palisades to downtown Los Angeles, to tape addresses

to the German people, but the project engaged him day and night.

The palm boulevards, the flowering gardens and orange groves, the blue of the Pacific, the yellow-green foothills, the constant sun, the immense vault of the star-studded sky, and the pervasive perfumed air—the remote innocence and gaiety of this environment was burdened with the weight of his heart. Evil could not triumph—that was his ultimate conviction.

"Oh, the sin of it!" Our buxom maid had once shouted to the Baltic winds, and she raged on. Our summer house did not exist for us any more; it had become a week-end cottage and hunting lodge for the Reichs Marshal. He had exterminated the beloved "sacred" elks. And the people of our chosen country were bombing Papa's native town and the home of our childhood—and we had to be grateful to them. My brothers wrote cheerful-serious letters from the front; friends were being killed. At night in Pacific Palisades we heard the macabre baying of coyotes. . . . And one day there was peace. Even if it was only because the Titans, whose lava had never ceased to shake the earth, were growing weary. . . .

❀❀❀

Let me only hint at my belief that the odd elegance of that distant shore, with its almost intangible beauty and worldly barrenness, which surrounded my father for twelve years had a great influence on him and on his work. It drove him from his own traditions to stylistic daring and gave him the courage for those linguistic experiments in *The Holy Sinner* and the thoroughly polemic "major confession" of *Dr. Faustus*. Also, although the book had already been written in Europe, this landscape served to bring out the seemingly disreputable but essentially true self-parody of *Felix Krull*. The gleaming emptiness, monotony, and hostility of the landscape ruthlessly threw men—especially those of artistic temper —back on their own resources, so that, mirrored in this almost supernatural setting, their individual essence came to the fore.

His life in California always puzzled him, even when his indiscriminate sensibilities found joy and usefulness in it. And he did not want to be buried there. In his old age he experienced a marvelous flowering there, yet all the time he may have secretly been longing for more familiar ground. This wish was fulfilled. His last years were spent in a more homelike atmosphere—he had breathed enough for-

❀❀❀

eign air. It was cozier and more friendly among the orchards, meadows, and forests at Kilchberg, on the shores of the picturesque "Zürisee." He could watch the fine cattle in the pastures, and listen to the peasants calling to one another. There my father lies buried. His grave looks out on that peaceful countryside, just as he had imagined it. As the dreams and ideals which lay at the root of his life had been realized in his work, so here too, a wish was fulfilled.

❀❀❀

[VII]

Our sojourn in the United States was only an episode, yet it forms one of the cornerstones of our existence—or better, it cements the cornerstones. The unreal character of our age cannot be denied—its hyper-rational spirit of inquiry; man's intrusion into the cosmos at the same time that he analyzes himself into dust—and since the unreal is inescapably in the air it is an advantage to observe it at close range on the continent where it is centered and where it manifests itself most freely. The more you avoid or ignore a phenomenon of your time, the more its dangerous distortion will haunt you; it is truly better to face it manfully. To have lived in the United States is, for us Europeans, nothing less than a revelation. I would be a benighted fool not to admit it or to want, with pious pride, to put my world above yours, since both are one world. We are so closely tied to each other, we depend so on one another, it would be grotesque to try to effect a separation. I may smile, smile anxiously, but I will not make fun of "the other side," as some inveterate Europeans do; their grandchildren may already think differently.

First and foremost it was my mother—this child-like, colorful, sturdy person—who in spite of a great deal of inborn conservatism revealed much "modernity" and found much pleasure in the new world. Though well along in her sixties, she enjoyed rushing along the highways in the open-top Ford or Buick, matching all "speed demons" in swiftness and dexterity. She enjoyed shopping in the gigantic supermarkets, where mothers bought large quantities of "cans" which were then loaded into their baby carriage until the baby seemed just another squalling item of canned goods. Then they would all return to their neat bungalows, each with its squared-off flowerbeds, standing in identical rows of hundreds. Inside these homes everything is practical and clean; you are your own boss and needn't be terrorized by servants! Even our large, elegant "Pacific Palisades" was servantless from time to time—whenever the

❀❀❀

Filipino, Japanese or Negro couples were all "off
the market." And suddenly my mother—who previously had been totally ignorant of the art—could
cook, and cooked excellently. She handled the shiny,
clever gadgets with childish pride and glee, and
these household worries did not cause her to neglect
her many other affairs and duties, especially helping
my father. Love and ambition were not missing in
her attitude toward social engagements: for those
Hollywood dinner parties were not to be taken
lightly. There has never been a place like the Hollywood of that era, a place of giants—writers, poets,
virtuosi, composers, conductors, actors of every na-
tionality—where each reigned alone, oddly isolated
on his throne. And those olympian parties—miracu-
lously brilliant though they were—provided only a
tenuous communication line between them.

I cannot forget the huge, solemn Bowl concerts,
the confluence of thousands and thousands of cars,
the unbroken mass of people (never have I seen such
an orderly, attentive crowd as here), the oversized
amphitheater, the iridescently illuminated shell in
which the orchestra sat, and the Haydn symphony
sounding against desert hills under a vast, starry
sky. . . . When we attended "en famille" (my young-

❀❀❀

est brother, by the way, sat in the shell with his viola), my mother did her bit by directing the car cleverly and fearlessly through the nightmarish traffic.

And today, in her seventies, does she shy away from the ocean waves? I still see my parents before me, on the boardwalk at Santa Monica under the brilliant noon sky, both in white, Papa in a Panama and wearing dark glasses, holding the black poodle on a red leash. Sedately, staunchly, they promenade arm in arm among the palms and bright flowerbeds, Mama throwing glances of childish desire at the foaming blue waves: it *would* be nice. . . .

There dwelled in her something impetuous, a natural drive, which she subordinated to her vocation as wife and mother. She fulfills this vocation more out of a sense of respect for destiny, and from a deep sense of duty, than because of basic inclination; and for this her life is all the more admirable. Dressed in her evening clothes and conversing at a fashionable party, my mother seemed only to be pretending, because she had been ordered to. In actuality, she would have been happier running through the winds across the moor, wearing a linen smock. Or, driving the car through the smart shopping district, she would love

❀❀❀

to go into fifth gear and fly away over the people and the housetops. Or while Papa is dictating his letters to her, she would like to be studying higher mathematics or rushing through Siberia on a sleigh hung with bells. While attending one of Papa's lectures (Wife of the Writer, seated in the front row), she longs to sink into the earth and join in the pranks of the nature spirits. . . . How secretly and elfishly being and longing seem separated here!

But, in the last analysis, no one unwillingly can spend fifty years being something which he is not; and so, in the final analysis, my mother wanted *this* life.

But now that she is alone, this inner power may be of use to her. At home in Kilchberg—where the poodle Niko (a similar dog though not the same) peeks through the folding doors from the living room into the study, looking with large, golden, questioning eyes at the desk, his tail wagging—at home in Kilchberg, let her be strong, and let good spirits watch over her. And there, too, is my oldest sister, who has always stood at my parents' side. And there are the grandchildren, on whom my mother dotes and who dote on her.

❀❀❀

[VIII]

My literary period came during the American years. At that time I was intoxicated with Tolstoy, Dostoevski, Gogol, Turgenev, Goethe, and Balzac; Fontane, Dickens, Shakespeare, and Dante; the German romantics, de Maupassant, Whitman, contemporary Americans. . . . I read and read, hundreds of volumes in a number of languages, which I bought in second-hand book stores and with which I decorated my various furnished rooms.

A number of languages—how rewarding languages are! Know one of them and soon you are on the track of language itself. When a piano piece is being transposed for the violin, the transcription or transposition passes through a non-instrumental stage in which it is "absolute music." While transposing the music, I hear it simultaneously on two different instruments, yet as one. With languages a similar phenomenon occurs—between the different languages lies the non-articulate realm of "absolute speech." I could go on to say that between the languages of the various arts—painting, music, poetry—lies a common area of "absolute art," and that in this exalted realm all the arts meet. Thus an artist, although master of only one art, has some knowledge of them all. My father, for example, thought a great deal about this absolute connection between the arts, and his understanding of music resounds in his work.

It is not my intention to write an essay on my father's work. It would hardly become me, nor would I have the ability to do so. Thousands may know his work better than I, and more than once I have been embarrassed in conversations about it. When it was a question of textual knowledge, or even of keen apperception of literary influences, I took refuge in ignorance—which, it is true, was in part pretended. Such conversations make me feel stupid and at the same time under a kind of fundamental attack. The roots of my being seemed outrageously to implore me: please, please be quiet.

❀❀❀

I haven't read more of him than of any other writer,
but I do feel an organic alliance with this work as
with no other.

When my father sent a copy of *Dr. Faustus* from
Pacific Palisades to me in Manhattan, he inscribed
it, "For Moni. She'll understand it all right." The
statement contains a fleeting, already dismissed dis-
dain, whose place is taken at once by trust. And my
own view corresponds to that of the dedication:
to put it paradoxically, without deep knowledge I
knew the work to its depths. My father said that
style is accommodation to the subject. Good. But his
style soars beyond, outshines his subject. That
sounds as if he were a virtuoso. He is. But—thinking
of passages in the Joseph series or in *Death in Venice*
—this preeminence of form results in a kind of virtu-
osity that is moving, beautiful, and inspired. I mean
to say that my father's work is more inspired form
than formed spirit. It is not true that life and work
are separate things; they are—and especially for him
—one. Was not his life, like his great work, dominated by form, so much so that it seemed to be more
existing form than formed existence? Form was not
a tool he used, it was basic to him. Order, courtesy,
moderation, patience were not means but essence, to

which he imparted life and meaning. What profound order was implicit in his life and his death! Sunday bells rang at his birth, and the festive peals of his natal day echo into his death. All the high honors that were bestowed on him at the last, all the public and private thanks and recognition—this final hymn to him was also on a Sunday. And between that first and this last Sunday lay a week of hard work.

[IX]

In the same sense that I spoke of absolute art, New York is the absolute city. It is the ideal city in which all other cities are dissolved: city as an abstraction. The architecture, the lighting, the pace, the climate, the size, the cosmopolitanism—these are components we can list, but much remains that is mysterious. Lying on the sofa in one cell of a rooming house with the blinds drawn, one has an intimation of the bright, hard, clear, intangible, tense, classic nature of this city of cities. Rising, going to the window, opening the blinds, and looking out, one no longer intuits it, but knows that one is a part of it. And walking through Central Park, along Fifth Avenue, on Broadway or one of the many, many parallel streets, one is an unconscious part of it. Yet there is little solidarity among its inhabitants, because their systematized, independent life almost excludes fellowship or human contact. Instead there is an unconscious, strong feeling of belonging in this city, as in no other. The systematized existence which separates people from each other and makes them solitary, provides a kind of protection for all. Oh, yes, in New York one can feel alone as in no other city; but at the same time one is protected as though by a gigantic, steely, abstract mother. All unaware, we draw from the city not only the strength for that harsh solitude, but sometimes an incomprehensible feeling of happiness.

When a tiny almond tree raises its naked branches against the skyscrapers, all bathed in pale light; when hundreds of feet shuffle up the subway steps and pale faces rise up blindly—blind to all others, focusing only on their own goals; when everything, untouched by warmth, strives strictly forward; when suddenly across the Hudson the light changes and almond trees, blind faces, and skyscrapers are dipped in sunset glow and a siren shrieks like sheer deliverance: then one is absorbed and sheltered in this great element, and desires to hold on to it and

❀❀❀

to bless it, so incomprehensible are its pride and its beauty.

This city, which by European standards may be prosaic, unpoetic, "cold," has its own rigid, proud poetry—as we already know from Walt Whitman and the music of Gershwin. We are caught up in its melody which, in spite of its complexity, seems to be played on one string. It is the melody of a hectic monotony, an iron melancholy, a conspiracy with today, with the moment. And because yesterday and tomorrow seem not to exist, the present is always mighty and pure like a young lion in a vacuum. Without memory, without true ambition, one lives in the present. Dollars are earned and spent, a woman is married and traded in for another, paper plates are used for meals and then consigned to the garbage pail, professions are chosen and changed, cars are bought and sold. . . . Just never make a commitment, be free, without ties, without tradition: the city's tradition is today. And if we lament something that happened day before yesterday, we are told, "That was a long time ago, that's over and done with, let's forget it, let's start anew!"

That isn't just an abstract attitude, but a point of

view which New Yorkers command and put into practice. Not that New York is totally without friendliness—but for the most part it is superficial, empty, much too casual. So a really genuine friendship is worth its weight in gold, and, accompanied by a friend, one can even smile at those almost offensively colorless get-togethers that take place at one end or the other of the metropolis. They are convocations where there is much drinking and little talk, where the television set furnishes the major entertainment, where the guests stand around as if they were meeting on the street, where the host steadily prepares more ice cubes in the kitchen, and where, without visible reason, no one leaves before two in the morning. Most of the time a "star"—a ballerina, a prize fighter, a Negro poet—is the attraction of the evening, but he generally disappears in the constellation of whiskey glasses and potato chips, absurdly patterned ties, checked sports jackets, nylon blouses, lipstick, and empty laughter. The odd thing is that one does persevere until two in the morning. These desolate parties are not without a certain grandeur, simply because they are organized, conscious, and willed. Usually one would go to a bar afterwards ("Let's have another drink!") and carry

❀❀❀

on until two twenty-five at the earliest. The sound of a fire-siren would awaken one early the next morning.

The energy of the people is fantastic. I know several who on Sunday would go to an early movie, would attend a concert in the afternoon, and in the evening would hear *Rosenkavalier* or *Tannhäuser*. Between these entertainments they sat *en famille* on the sofa, smoking Luckies and watching football on television, with a bottle of Scotch close by. On the way to the theater the car radio produced jazz music. And all the time they were in the best of spirits. In the office on Monday, the events of the previous day would already be forgotten.

Others spent weekends driving thousands of miles through the country to get to some gloomy, reedy lake where they would hold orgies in their trailers. "Keep smiling!" It was magnificent. Isn't such energy magnificent?

I knew an invalid boy who was kept alive by insulin injections and who worked the night shift in a factory. He was called Happy, and he was. Most people, in addition to their jobs, have a "hobby." This ailing, cheery night worker spent his days carving toys from bamboo and match boxes. A gas-station attendant may be a saxophone player on the side, a dentist may paint abstractions, a policeman study psychology, a department-store clerk go to drama school, an elevator operator be a quiz show contestant, a secretary a coloratura, a drugstore counterman an ice-skating champion, a piano tuner an astrologer, a bus driver a nightclub comic. To make money is one thing; to keep oneself entertained, another. This separation often leads to an inner split, may even lead to schizophrenia; and this, in turn, justifies the army of psychoanalysts.

The energy poured into work is enormous. Whether a man is an advertising artist, college professor, radio announcer, baker, Wall Street functionary, sports promoter, art dealer, surgeon, or farmer —he lives under an enormous strain (though this is relieved by routine): the utmost is demanded and given. A little office girl types like lightning; provincial orchestras perform with electrifying precision; each "show girl" works like a machine. Perfection—in spite of quantity—is the order of the day (if only superficially, aiming less for the particular than for the general). A favorite expression of approval is "Perfect!" whether it concerns a play, a joke, a dish, a woman, or the weather. Implicit in

❀❀❀

the word is approbation for a new high in achieve-
ment. Material comforts, sanitation, and the high
standard of living do not decrease these exertions. The
subway, the riders packed in like cattle, or the lunch
hours in the crowded, deafening cafeterias, or the
indescribable summer heat: these alone are enough
to put people on their mettle. The New Yorker's
"keep smiling" steels him; and the "keep smiling"
seems made of steel.

[X]

I have taken many journeys. The one to my parents in California led straight across the continent. Four days and four nights across the emptiness, across the plains broken by jagged, snow-covered mountain ranges under the shining heavens. I remember that sometimes during these journeys I felt empty and happy, as if I were dreaming, as if there were no beginning or end anywhere against which one might strike, as if there were no need or pain anywhere, as if I were only the shell of myself, senselessly and weightlessly conquering time and space. I traveled to the Carolinas, through New England to Vermont and New Hampshire, through the state of New York, and everywhere I found beautiful, warm, European scenes, with wooded hills, flower-strewn meadows, and picturesque lakes. But in the midst of these landscapes there often lay something gigantic and frightening—like an enormous turkey farm, full of fluttering, noise, and hellish stench; or a vast flying field where outsize metal insects flashed in the sun, endless and terrifying; or a huge home for the aged, where thousands of old people passed their days.

Twice a year my parents came to New York. Sometimes I met my brothers or sisters there, and I had some particularly intimate visits from my late eldest brother. My youngest sister also dropped in now and again, with her briefcase, from Chicago. I breakfasted with my eldest sister while she lay in bed after finishing a lecture tour of fifty-two cities. My youngest brother paid me a visit, on his way from San Francisco to Germany with his violin, and we spent a blissful evening over red wine.

I had happy days chatting comfortably with my parents in streamlined hotels. At dinner Papa, as usual, would stick to soup (which he would spoon rhythmically, with visible enjoyment, while it was still very hot) and to ice cream; for many years he had been bored, almost annoyed, by the main course. He took pleasure in the waiters' German, which was apt to be, though fluent, fairly comical, and with a naively surprised and yet joyous smile he would give his autograph to someone who had come to our table. Between courses he smoked long, somewhat effeminate Reeges cigarettes, and he had no hesitation about drinking two cups of strong coffee. At tea time he sat in his dimly-lit suite, with its thick pile carpet, strawberry-red armchairs, and gold-framed mirrors which reflected the somewhat hollow splendor of gladioli. Here he would receive a publisher, a reporter, a friend, or a stranger who had convinced my mother on the telephone that he "must see The Master for ten minutes." After expressing his adulation, such a person would ask either for a thousand dollars or for "personal advice," or would pull a fat manuscript from his briefcase with the request that my father promote it. When my father read it, he would recognize that it was a piece of nonsense. The stranger, with anguish written on his face, would come to tea once more. Then my father would give him back his manuscript with a smile of sincere regret, with a small present of money, and with the polite advice that he try poultry raising—art just wasn't everybody's métier. Besides, it might very well be that one day on his poultry farm he might turn out a nice little story.

Once we were walking along Fifth Avenue in the direction of Central Park, just as later we would walk along the Via Veneto in Rome in the direction of the Villa Borghese—the two sophisticated districts are similar. The day was fiercely hot. Papa walked very straight, Panama and walking cane in hand. Perhaps his shoulders sagged just a little, and his neck might have been thrust forward just a bit as he ran his eyes along the buildings and stood still. He pulled the violet-scented handkerchief from the pocket of the summer suit (which, though "off the rack," hung very elegantly on him) and guided it to his forehead, carefully patting. Then he walked on, seemingly braced and contented. But the shoulders really did sag a little, and his neck *was* inclined a little to one side—he seemed a little sad, a little on guard, a little withdrawn in the face of this city's power. What was the upper-class boy from Lübeck doing here, how had he got here? What was the bond between that ancient, crookedly gabled, but sturdy little harbor town and these massive yet soaring, naked, upward-yearning piles of steel and stone? One does not ask. One is simply here. It happened this way—because of "historical necessity," whims of fate, secret willfulness. . . . Many things coincided knocked down a lady. Although it frightened her, she looked after him with sympathy, almost enraptured. Why? And in the collision she had lost a glove, and no one picked it up for her. Later she would discover the loss and think back on that gentleman. She would smile anew, enraptured. . . . Papa unfolded the violet-handkerchief and patted his neck and face: the heat was absurd.

In Stockholm and Copenhagen it would be cooler, in Amsterdam, London, Hamburg, and in Sils. Once a year my father traveled abroad, like a virtuoso. He recited, collected a decoration or honorary doctorate here and there, and returned home to Pacific Palisades. There he continued uninterrupted to write his novels and dream of a chalet in Switzerland.

Now, in the midst of hot, clamorous New York, he was suddenly dazzled, as by a Christmas tree. He stood before a display of silver. There was a large, splendid store window full of enchantingly flashing, blinking, shimmering, glimmering, glittering, glowing, gleaming objects—the kind of things my father had always loved so well. It fascinated him. He stared at them, infatuated and full of longing. He was not to be moved on. My mother had to drag him away by the sleeve. It was a Sunday feeling, a fes-

❀❀❀❀

[XI]

After a twelve-year absence I saw Europe again.
Why did I return there? Did I return with the intention of divorcing myself from America? I left the
United States quite ingenuously, left behind my be-
longings—books and household things—as well as a
large part of myself. This is a continent one can't
just shed. And although for years now I have been
taking root again in the "old world," to which I was
ineluctably drawn, I have not parted with America
to this day.

Its vast, anonymous, childlike spirit is a revelation. It refreshes one's feeling. My sight and my
heart were expanded by it, rendered more open and
more free, more critical and more thankful for the
whole world. The comparisons, the parallels that

meet in infinity broaden one's horizon and produce
a greater loyalty—but also a greater melancholy, because now the child knows what is hidden behind
the curtain, and curiosity and illusion are doomed.
Lately I have met Italians and Germans who have
said to me, scornfully or longingly, "I'd like to see
America sometime!" And I have wanted to reply,
"Go on, go; all your ridiculous or splendid presup-
positions will collapse and a new reality will stand
before you like a force, a fortress."

We laughed a little at our emotion, my youngest
brother and I, when we spied Genoa rising before us.
It appeared like a vision; and as its landmarks, its
palaces, its colorful harbor grew ever clearer before
our eyes, the returning exiles on board our ship wept
and sang and shouted. It was good that we laughed
a little at ourselves, for just as the excessively happy
or the excessively sad easily becomes comic, so too
the grotesque was not lacking in this deeply emotional moment. While our hearts were beating and
tears rising to our eyes, we stood as if paralyzed
among our innumerable pieces of luggage surrounded by the excited crowd, chaotic customs
problems, interpreters, tourist guides, beggars, children, and rogues who wanted our money and roused

❀❀❀

our anger. Finally we gave ourselves up to gentle madness, refused all "help," and eventually found shelter in a dubious hotel where we prepared, between tears and laughter, for the first night home.

God must enjoy throwing pepper on the great moments, and He does well to do it. They do not diminish because of it, but proudly assert themselves under the fiery spice. It is the interweaving and the counterplay of the values in a thing that make up its total value. And there was an interweaving and counteracting of sensations in me at the beginning of my return. In me, there raged a "divine confusion of feelings," and I suffered. But perhaps I enjoyed this suffering. The familiar, seen in a new perspective and removed into another time—with all that I had experienced and that had happened to me dancing like bright shadows behind it—made me dizzy. It brought me simultaneously pain and joy, heaviness and tenderness, disappointment and fulfillment; it appeared small and vain, measured against the dreams we had had in exile; so I could hug it to myself like a toy fallen from the heavens into my lap.

And yet the familiar seemed to have turned to stone in a world full of motion and change. Only

❀❀❀

slowly did the "toy" take on size and dignity. Our tensions began to relax; our senses, where days and weeks had been tangled as in a thorny hedge, were set free. Slowly, we achieved order and calm. It could not happen without some compromise. For I found myself unable, in the "old world," to choose my native country as my abode. I went to Italy, which had been for many years the home of my heart.

I don't believe the compromise implies either resentment or renunciation, but a natural, honest disposition. It would have been presumptuous to try to return to the past; foreign lands had become too much my home. And nowhere but in Italy is the foreign so homey. The exoticism of its landscape, its towns, its people, its language, contains so much music and evokes such unconscious recognition that one feels one has really reached home. There you find so much that is naive and authentic, so much undemanding, natural worth, so much that is child-like and yet ancient, so much nature and history, so much pride and modesty, so much poverty and so much happiness. I am speaking here less of the motorized, ambitious cities (though even these are still "authentic," and in the end incorruptible). I made me fearful. Not only because so much of it had been destroyed or changed and because I knew almost no one there any more, but also because my own shuddering spirit lay in the streets like an apple to be squashed. Deep feelings are better experienced at home, unseen; but I experienced them publicly, cruelly exposed and cruelly unrecognized, so that I was ashamed in front of people. Ashamed, but also tempted to catch at their sleeves, to whisper into their ears, to give them a flaming report, and then to say aloud, "You see, now you know, my good man." Even his tyrolean hat and loden coat might now strike me as soothingly initiate, and his hobnailed steps, receding on the pavement, steeled my heart. I don't know what imp drove me suddenly to address a newsboy in broken German and ask him directions to a well-known square. He gave them to me in his way—more well-meaning than explicit—and I bought his most exotic paper and took off in the direction of the square. When I got there and sat down in a café and read the paper, I could no longer distinguish my game from truth, for in large part I really felt a foreigner. It was November; there was a thick fog. I took a taxi because the trolley numbers were no longer the same, and this put me off. The

cabbie drove like a maniac. When I got out and paid
him, he said, "So we made it after all." "Did I say
there was any hurry?" I asked him, amused and
horrified by the breakneck ride. "We made it," he
repeated, obdurate and cheerful. I could only see
fog, and a house I didn't recognize.

The windows were empty except for one, in which
sat a painter splashing whitewash on the walls with
a great brush. Witlessly, I stared up at him. He
grinned. I grinned back, whereupon he asked, seriously, almost morosely, "Are you moving in here?"
"I think not." "You think not?" No, I said, and anyway I wasn't from this city. I walked on. As I passed
the house again, the painter had descended to the
street. Now he wore a dark jacket over his white
trousers. As he swung a leg across his bicycle he
turned his young face to me and called, "Hello,
Miss." I wanted to call back, "Wait!" But he had
already disappeared.

That strange house in the heavy fog stood on the
site of my parents' house. The garden fence was still
there, a little weathered but unmistakably *our* garden fence. Through the slats I could see that the
birches were gone, and the rose beds and lilac
bushes—not even the chestnut tree was left: only the

❀❀❀

pergola remained, and all kinds of rubbish was heaped about. I could have gone in; no one was there. But I didn't—everything was so sad and meaningless. It hurt, this lack of meaning. But something in me rejoiced. Why? Because I was standing there, at the gloomy, faded, disguised site of my childhood, and saw and felt—coat collar turned up, forehead wrinkled, leaning a little on my umbrella like a general who, leaning on his saber, looks over the ruins of the battlefield. I went to The Chauffeurs, a tavern above the river where, as children, we had sometimes stopped in for a glass of beer or lemonade. I crossed the bridge behind which stood the bulbous-towered church whose bells had always rung with severity and doom as we walked to school. The bells were ringing again, like a parody, across the decades.

And I went into the English Garden, where handsome dogs and pleasant children romped among the fogged-in trees and where a brand-new merry-go-round, whirling emptily to its barrel-organ music, suggested a ride; and I ran into an old school friend to whom I told the story of my life in five minutes; and I went to a performance of *Freischütz*, and refreshed myself with the terrors of the Wolves' Gorge,

❀❀❀

as in my childhood. . . . And I visited an old aunt and the National Museum, and in between these I "appeared" on the radio and felt foolish. What was to be said, since it was all a dream? And I locked myself into my hotel room and decided that I did not want to stay here, that I would be satisfied with the dream and depart before I woke up.

I don't mean to say that my encounter with my birthplace was a disappointment—it was a test I set myself and passed. Had I settled there, I should probably have failed it.

❀❀❀

[XII]

Rome is a beautiful city. It is true that I am put off by the caravans of those who devour beauty with binoculars and darken the sun. I myself have ridden in a carriage through Casablanca or Verona and after only two hours thought that I owned it all: the veiled women in the bazaars, the doelike, dark children with the beseechingly outstretched hands, the realm of the Sultan with his magic gardens, the white mosques against the azure sky, and the mules on the shimmering cliffs over the light blue sea. And I thought I knew the attractive, ceremonial little town of Romeo and Juliet. But I know only too well that we must grow familiar with beauty, need to win it, find that it will not let us overpower it. I know that I would have to live a long time in the oriental splendor of Venice, with its musty odors, and its ghostly, intimate web of alleys and voices, before I knew it.

And Rome? Perhaps a hundred years would be enough to comprehend its richness. I did not throw myself into it, but let it slowly make its way with me —somewhat like rarefied mountain air or an old wine. In my abbess's chamber the noises of the city were distant, and before my windows wisteria hung like heavily perfumed grapes. The former convent looked over flat roofs where buxom girls sang while hanging up the washing to dry. The motors and bells, the sharp, almost brutal voice of Rome here sounded unreal.

Here I wrote my "saucy little pieces" as my father called them, and sorted out my thoughts at the great table which was much too large and respectable for me. But in Rome substance and dignity are rather like a large, holy animal that allows itself to be petted. The mighty, ancient objects—palaces, pillars, temples, fountains, gardens, and ruins—in spite of the weight of their thousand years, are still full of contemporaneity, still full of life's motley, glowing tumult, so that all the time from the city's beginning to the present seems to fall within one uninterrupted

❀❀❀

day. And so it is quite proper that here the old should stand shoulder to shoulder with the new, that stream-lined cars should stand in front of the Pantheon, that streamlined ladies and monks conversing in Latin should all be walking on the Pincio.

My parents came to Rome. My father had not seen it for exactly fifty years and reveled in youthful memories. There was the very tavern where he and his brother Heinrich used to have long conversations with the owner. There were the Spanish steps where the two boys had quoted from Goethe's *Italian Journey* and sketched caricatures. And here was the theater where Wagner had been hissed amid cries of "Viva Verdi!" There was the Villa Adria, and Ostia Antica—those urban fragments in the landscape, with their pure shapes and visions in mosaic, where man's works had become part of nature. . . .

"Roma!" My father hurled forth the word with that classic Italian open "o," and with the sound evoked all its meaning. Proud tradition and child-like belief in eternity were part of it. He knew how to produce many such sounds without knowing the language, and that was enough; the sound alone fully conveyed the atmosphere of the city which he so devoutly loved. This love was prob-

ably more artistic than personal, a feeling fused
of art and religion, an obeisance to eternal values. When we were walking on the Aventino,
that noblest and most solemn of the seven hills,
and looked down on Vatican City lying in spring-
time splendor, the staunch, northern Protestant
would joke, "If I lived here, I'd probably turn Catholic." And it wasn't all that much of a joke, either.
He was expressing those universal and all-embracing
qualities that seemed to transfigure his old age. And
he must have meant to say that—from a purely symbolic point of view, unblemished by reality—here
stood a single and high fortress in the midst of a
torn world.

This incident probably made him decide to request an audience of the Pope. It was granted him,
and to the end of his life he was filled with it. Will
I ever forget how he sat in the lobby of my hotel
and told of it? In his black suit (the tiny but bright
red badge of the Legion of Honor in his buttonhole)
he looked like one who has just passed a professional
examination or like a participant in a high tragedy
upon which the curtain had just rung down. He told
his story like a boy who is in the throes of a magnificent dream—or rather, who has just seen a mag-

nificent dream come true. A boy who really had been allowed to wander from one golden room to another—just as his dream foretold—and who had been finally assigned a place among important men (now the proceedings were rather like those in the waiting room of an eminent physician), only to be summoned at once and to be led by a Swiss Guard and a cardinal through the last, final doorway to stand face to face with the Holy Father.

"He walked toward me. I wasn't meant to approach him, and he stood throughout our conversation. He always conducts his audiences standing. It seemed completely natural to me when I took leave of him to bend my knee and kiss his ring. I knelt to the ages."

In Pope Pius XII—who happened to be the same age as my father, though in delicate and failing health, and whose spirit and will triumphed again and again over physical debility—in him my father saw a symbolic brother, one who like himself represented the world of the spirit.

❀❀❀

[XIII]

It rises in waves, eddies thunderingly, breaks foaming against the rocks, shatters in spray against the sky—the sea!

On my island autumn has come. It is hardly noticeable, for the sun is hot—except that a golden tint has been added to its white glow. The Indian fig trees and cactuses are in their full glory; grapes, shiny with dew, invite the palate. Only the air has become a little more still although the winds blow harder, and there is something more reserved about the dawn—it no longer seems a greeting to mankind. People are far away and soon they will be further still, and we will stand alone on the cliffs and look out to sea. And we will go into the *campagna* and look for brushwood, cry our own names into the wind, and when the sun sets and the winter clouds flame in the west like an annunciation we will merge with them in a single heartbeat. And then the sound of bells will rise. But there will be no bell-ringer. All is far away, even the bell-ringer is far away, we are alone on the island!

And during our walk home, a branch catches in my hair. Then we stop and twist and twist the branch. And then you laugh. Why? Now I have to laugh too. It is already getting dark—and we laugh. At home the brushwood burns in the fireplace, and behind us the misty night is burning. . . .

Often in winter my island seems to be without people. Its inhabitants are in the villages. Out there, by the flowering cliffs, there is no one left.

The lower village is like a sophisticated toy, with its little alleys and fancy little stores where the wares are spread out as in a bazaar. There you make your way between colorful baskets and gilt sandals, between brilliant jewelry and abstract hairdressers' mannequins, plucked chickens, fruits, candy, and handwoven stoles. It is a vain, burrowing hamlet, a microcosm that cares nothing for the great world. Between the lower village and the upper village there is contempt. The upper village is the rougher brother, built on vine-growing soil, and full of tumbledown taverns and barefooted types. There lives an old bearded woman who sells live sardines and teaches prayers and curses to the small, ragged boys. Between the two villages, half way on the road, passersby cross themselves—a mishap presumably once took place there. Each of the villages has its patron saint, one in shiny silver, the other made of wood. On his feast day the silver saint weaves at the front of a long procession that winds its way to the blare of trumpets through sunny shore paths looking toward the islands and the volcanic city lying in the distant blue haze. The wooden saint is carried around the vineyard, followed by the ragged boys and the bearded old woman, and it is impossible to tell if she is singing, cursing, or praying as she raises her knobby dark hands to the sky.

But on both the upper and the lower *piazza* the bearded men stand every day—their trousers rolled up, wearing wooden clogs on their feet and berets on their curly heads, sucking on pipes—and let the sun shine on them. When it rains they stand in doorways and stare forlornly at the *piazza*.

Unless the sea is raging, they are out there, in their broad old boats that are shiny with black oil and whose weathered, rust-colored sails lean proudly and picturesquely in the wind. The men take their catch of octopus and squid to the volcanic city, and with the proceeds they buy bread for their women and their nineteen children. Sometimes the children wander hand in hand to the flowering cliffs. They seem to be searching and collecting something. They clamber up and down like lizards, and disappear, and the cliffs stand alone against the blue sky.

There is an empty house, jutting into the water like a long, red ship. We stand up there, leaning against each other, surrounded by the emerald waves, and watch the gulls. Their wings motionless, they stand in the air like white falcons or eagles, spy out the ground, and suddenly hurl themselves down with a cry. It is no longer lonesome here. The sea laps around the island like a cherished visitor from afar. And this island realm is like a single, high, shining fortress in the midst of a torn world. . . .

At the beginning of the new year, music is played on the *piazza*, and the people dance. They wear red pirates' costumes, and even on the church steps they dance and sing—even tiny little children and graybeards. And we dance, too. Then we lie on the cliffs, under the still, white houses set in their cactus gardens. And we watch the lizards as they dance in the sun.

❀❀❀